SHATTERED PULPITS: SHOULD YOUR PASTOR BE FIRED?

BY

BRIAN D. BEVERLY II

Shattered Pulpits: Should Your Pastor Be Fired

Published by Outpour Press
P.O. 4014
Hammond, LA 70404

ISBN-10: 0-578-43726-0
ISBN-13: 978-0-578-43726-2

Printed in the USA

Edited by Amanda Beverly

DEDICATION

For my wife Amanda, who has been one of my
greatest inspirations. You are the love of my life and I
am eternally grateful for you.

For my children, Kamden, Ada, Bailey, and Micaiah.
You are God's gifts to me and your mother.

For the Church of the Lord Jesus Christ! May the
Church continue to push back the darkness.
.

TABLE OF CONTENTS

INTRODUCTION

I love the Church of Jesus Christ because, when understood Biblically, the Church is the most amazing, dynamic, spectacular, supernatural, powerful, beautiful, loving, grace-filled, and life-transforming entity on planet earth. And it has always been this way. There are many churches that are operating as Christ intended. However, there are also many churches in America and abroad that have been tainted. Why is this? Well, one major reason is that they have been polluted with pastors that have disqualified themselves or were never called by God. Indeed there are churches whose pastors have agendas other than Christ's agenda. Therefore, under the leadership of debunked pastors, some churches are hobbled, crippled, and lack the power Christ intended.

Have you ever been to a church and felt like there was an agenda that might not have been Christian? Have you ever been to a church that feels more like a business instead of the house of God? Have you ever been to a church that felt more like a social club than a church equipping the saints for ministry? Could it be that the reason a church may not be achieving its Christian purpose is because the pastor behind the pulpit is steering the congregation another direction?

This book is going to ask the question that some may not want to delve into. In fact, some may think only qualified PhD's or Christian leaders in the upper echelon should consider such a question. But now more than ever, we need Christians of all maturity levels to be discerning. The question being, "Are we allowed to ask if a pastor is really called and sent by God?" I believe the answer is "yes." I also believe denominations and other Christian organizations/associations have asked this question of their perspective ministers, but often in their asking, they have failed to truly discern if a person is called to be a pastor or not. Beyond organizations and denominations, I have even noticed that the overall population of Christians is failing to discern if a pastor is truly called by God or not. Basically, just because a pastor is nice, charming, talented, educated, or has a certain style doesn't mean they are called by God. Even Jesus told us there would be false prophets (Matthew 7:15-20).

This book is for every Christian to be equipped to discern who is a true Christian leader or not. This book is for perspective Christian leaders in training at seminaries, Bible colleges, or under mentorship, for them to really ask themselves if God has called them. This book is for current pastors/Christian leaders, to evaluate if their agenda for a church is in line with God's agenda. This book is going to provide perspective and healing for both the church attender and the pastor. The Church is such a wonderful place, there is so much hope for the Church, and God is bringing integrity back to the pulpit!

·

ONE

THE HIRELING

Years ago when I was in seminary, I attended a ministry conference that a pastor friend invited me to. My friend was an associate pastor at the church hosting the conference and said there was a youth pastor position opening up and he wanted me to meet the lead pastor who would be the main speaker that night. Before the conference began the lead pastor was mingling and connecting with different people in the crowd. My friend saw this as an opportunity to introduce me. Upon shaking the lead pastor's hand and looking into his eyes, I felt disturbed on a spiritual level. I felt like there was something off with his character. It was as if the Lord said to me, "You do not want to connect with this man!"

I tried not to make much of the negative impression or thoughts about this pastor. So, the conference began and the worship team was amazing, even the lead pastor's sermon was well spoken, Biblical, thoughtful, and energetic. However, as I drove home that night I could not shake the feeling I had about the lead pastor. I knew in my spirit that I was not to pursue a ministry position or relationship with this pastor.

About a month and a half after the conference my friend approached me at school and said, "Brian, you're not gonna believe this!" "Try me," I said confidently. He replied, "My lead pastor…you know the one I introduced you to…it was recently revealed that he had been in an affair with one of the members of the church." When my friend gave me this information I yelled ecstatically, gleefully, and with a determined look on my face, "I KNEW IT…I KNEW IT." I confused my friend because he was quite somber and disappointed by the news, and yet, I was acting like an excited child who just found a piece of candy in their pocket. I explained to my friend that on the night I met his lead pastor, I could sense something was not right, and how this news just confirmed why God gave me such a disturbing feeling toward him.

Discernment

I want to speak to the Christian who has had a similar experience to mine (or one day will). You have had moments where you were around a supposedly "Christian environment," with people who claim to be "Christian," and yet, your spiritual sense told you "God is not involved here." However, you fight that sense sometimes because you do not want to be deemed as "Critical," "Self-righteous," "Judgmental," or "Holier than thou." But on the contrary, I would like to tell you that sometimes what you sense is directly from God. It is the Holy Spirit trying to warn you not to make a bad connection with the people or situations that would have a negative influence on you. The Holy Spirit will guide you to all truth (John 16:13), which includes revealing places and people that would affect you negatively (1 Corinthians 15:33).

Spiritual discernment is a gift from God (1 Corinthians 12:10) that allows the Christian to be able to perceive the spirit, nature, and motivation of a person or situation. Even when there is little to no physical evidence to give you a hint, the spiritually discerning person has a deep sense of the true nature of things seen or unseen, of what is of God or not of God—hence, they are able to make judgments based on their developed discernment of things. Some develop this gift at a deeper level than others. Nonetheless, at a basic level, all Christians should be able to discern the spirit of another person. We should be able to diagnose what is sanctioned by the Lord.

The fact of the matter is this, as Christians, we are to make judgement calls! If we are to exclusively point people to Jesus Christ with all certainty, then you will have to make a judgement call. Let me ask you a few questions: do you believe that salvation is found in Jesus Christ alone? The Apostles who walked closely with Jesus certainly did (Acts 4:8-12), even Jesus made the claim that He was the only way to God the Father (John 14:6). So if someone said there are multiple gods, and one does not need to accept or follow Jesus for salvation, would you agree with them? No, of course not! As a Christian, you would have to lovingly reject their claim and point them to Christ. In other words, you would have to make a judgement call! The Bible states that *"The person with the Spirit makes judgments about all things..."* (1 Corinthians 2:15a, NIV). The Apostle Paul taught we are to make judgements in the house of God (1 Corinthians 5:12). Even successful entrepreneurs, leaders, cooks, parents, and police officers have to make judgement calls.

The reason we struggle with judging is that we confuse making a judgement with condemning. It is not the Christian's job to convict or condemn anyone, that is reserved for God. However, we are to make judgments as they relate to the truth. Therefore if somebody claims that promiscuity, lying, and murder is the will of God, I need to make a judgement call as a Christian and boldly and lovingly stand for the truth and say, "that's wrong." If somebody says 1+1= 4, should we not judge their reasoning and say, "you're wrong?" If someone consumes too much alcohol and is a detriment to themselves and society, is it not loving to make a judgment call in light of the truth and say, "I'm sorry but your alcoholism is wrong?" It is the truth that sets people free and I am persuaded that there are hundreds if not thousands of people we encounter in our lives daily that are shackled by brokenness, despair, fear, and ignorance because we do not

8

love them enough to tell them the truth with grace on our lips.

It is wrong to make judgements for the sake of condemning someone, but it is right to make judgements for the sake of the truth, love, and redemption of a person. Judging for the sake of truth and redemption of someone's spirit is totally different from judging to make oneself God and send people to Hell—we are not the final authority on such matters. Nonetheless, as Christians, we judge, always hoping that people receive the same grace we received and did not deserve. God loves the world, and our judgments should reflect that.

God loves His people. He is a good Father. Any good parent wants to protect their children. So God has given us this powerful gift of discernment for our protection, so that we can judge wisely and effectively for the glory of God; so that we are not consumed by those that would do us harm. We have all heard people say, "If I would have known back then, what I know now, I would have chosen differently." And I want you to know, child of God, that discernment can protect you from making decisions you will later regret. You can utilize God's gift of discernment to avoid pitfalls. We cannot just be suspicious anymore, we have to hear from God and make wise judgements. *"Dear friends, do not believe every spirit, but test the spirits to see whether they are from God, because many false prophets have gone out into the world,"* (1John 4:1).

Why Shattered Pulpits?

Traditionally and even today, the pulpit has always been seen as a place of authority for the pastor. A pulpit can be understood as a podium or stand from which the preacher speaks. Whether a pulpit is a traditional looking podium, a music stand, a tall table, and so on…whatever the preacher uses to place notes upon and preach is considered a pulpit. The pulpit is not limited to a physical podium but also can include the space in which the pastor occupies while addressing a people or congregation. So even if the pastor does not have a podium to place notes on or to stand behind, the space in which the pastor preaches becomes the pulpit area. Hence, when we speak about the pulpit we are speaking about the pastor's authority given to them by God, to serve and speak Heavenly mysteries on behalf of God.

Now before going further I need to say that at this point if you are still struggling with the idea of discernment/ judging, then excuse me as I say what you may have sensed but never had the courage to say: "Dear Christians, sometimes you are right and they are wrong; you have the truth, but they are devoid of it." And for the purposes of this book, I need to tell you that not every pastor that is behind a pulpit or podium is from God. There are pastors behind pulpits with agendas not from God, and they are not only hurting themselves but God's people. Their position of authority behind the pulpit is false, it is a shattered pulpit, and unbeknownst to the people in their congregations the shards of these shattered pulpits—these false and debunked pastors—cut, damage, and even destroy the people that listen to them.

It is paramount to understand that there are some pastors behind pulpits today because they are messengers of Satan and have rotten intentions, some were never called by God but thought it was a good idea to become a pastor, others were called but because of sin and/or hurt feelings being allowed to control them, they have disqualified themselves —any conclusion you come to...the fact of the matter remains: their pulpits are shattered! There is no real authority from God when they speak or perform their duties.

Why The Term "Hireling?"

These debunked pastors operating behind shattered pulpits (false authority) are known as "Hirelings." The best definition of the Hireling is to say: They were either never called by God or they were once called by God but have now sold out for a price. Instead of being called by God they hire themselves out to the highest bidder. The price for which one sells out is different for each of these Hirelings. The price could be prestige, money, comfort, lust, political party agendas, self-righteousness exploits of vain imaginations that have caused them to chase a position behind a pulpit. We will talk about what a called pastor sent by God looks likes later, but in short, a pastor that belongs to God does not have a price—they simply want to accomplish the will of God in their lives and in the lives of others. However, the Hireling has a price. They do what they do because of their own will. They do things in the name of God, but God has not anointed them. For some God's anointing was on these Hirelings at one point, but for some reason of disqualification God removed His anointing/approval, and now the church suffers because the once legitimate pastor has lost God's approval, but they refuse to step down from this position of influence. Jesus talked about these Hirelings in the gospel of John:

"Very truly I tell you Pharisees, anyone who does not enter the sheep pen by the gate, but climbs in by some other way, is a thief and a robber. The one who enters by the gate is the shepherd of the sheep. The gatekeeper opens the gate for him, and the sheep listen to his voice. He calls his own sheep by name and leads them out. When he has brought out all his own, he goes on ahead of them, and his sheep follow him because they know his voice. But they will never follow a stranger; in fact, they will run away from

him because they do not recognize a stranger's voice. (John 10:1-6)

Jesus used this figure of speech against the Pharisees. In essence, He was claiming the Pharisees were illegitimate as religious leaders, they were not really put in position by God, nonetheless, it did not register with them. But what the Pharisees did not understand is plain for those who believe. Jesus is saying that some shepherds/pastors are inadequately taking care of God's sheep/congregation because they hopped the fence! They did not go through the proper channels, they have their own agendas, they did not go through the front gate, because they do not have a call from God, and therefore are not fit to take care of God's people.

I think more often than not we sense this. Within our spirits, we meet people who claim to be pastors but they are really just a Hireling who did not come in through the gate but hopped over the fence and claimed a position and title without the blessing of God. Unless such Hirelings are exposed on the media for egregious activities such as embezzlement or some type of sex scandal, we just ignore the unction of the Holy Spirit warning us about pastors who are posing and not fit to lead God's people.

In the following is an excerpt from my book *Wake Up Ladies: Reclaiming That Which Has Been Lost*, where I talk about unfit or disqualified pastors:

"In my first year of seminary, I wanted to get to know some of the seminary seniors. Hence, when there were three seniors sitting on the patio of the campus coffee shop I saw them and I thought to myself, "I would love to get to know them! Because they are getting ready to graduate they must be serious about their faith." I sat down with them at the table. The conversation was great. We talked about Christian doctrine, Church history, their favorite professors, and movies. Meanwhile, a seminary faculty member came by the table for a short conversation. She said some nice things and then proceeded to the coffee shop.

When she left, one of the seminary students started talking about her breasts and how infatuated he was with them. He even went as far as to make hand gestures about the size of her breasts. As for the other two seniors sitting at the table, they were laughing and agreeing with him. I sat in total shock. I could not believe that seniors, future pastors, would talk about this seminary faculty in this manner. She was a very modest woman. She never wore clothing that would draw this type of attention to her." (55-56).

I walked away from that table and there was a sick feeling in my gut. It was very clear that while these men were training and learning to be pastors, they were unfit for the task. They knew how to study, preach, counsel, and conduct meetings but did they actually have the calling, character, and commitment to be pastors at the time? The answer is a resounding, no! They were Hirelings which meant they could be bought or would eventually sell out for something other than Christ's agenda. In this case, they were bought by their lust. How dangerous it is to equip Hirelings to do the work of Jesus Christ. It is analogous to giving a murderer or terrorist a loaded gun. The only difference is a murderer just kills the body, but a Hireling can affect someone's eternity by destroying the spirit.

In John's gospel, Jesus goes on to say:

"I am the good shepherd. The good shepherd lays down his life for the sheep. The hired hand is not the shepherd and does not own the sheep. So when he sees the wolf coming, he abandons the sheep and runs away. Then the wolf attacks the flock and scatters it. The man runs away because he is a hired hand and cares nothing for the sheep." (John 10:11-13)

So not only have these Hirelings entered the sheep pen by climbing over the fence, but they run at the sight of trouble or tension because they are not committed to the sheep/congregation. At the end of the day, a Hireling will never pay a price higher than what they are comfortable with or what they really want. Because the Hireling will only do what is necessary for their own agenda and not God's agenda. They have sold out for something else.

While Hirelings deceive themselves into thinking their motives are noble, they are always looking for greener pastures for themselves and not for those they care for—the congregation. They think it is wise and smart to move from church to church every two to five years and recycle the exact same sermons around the calendar as they did at their last church. Each congregation is different, with different people and different needs, and the pastor should be trusting God for a new message that relates to the season of the current congregation. Moreover, to their discredit, the Hireling thinks it is wise to download sermons from other preachers instead of spending hours in prayer and study, searching the mind and heart of God on behalf of the people. There is a reason why the details of Moses' message is not the same message Jonah had for the Ninevites. If you are familiar with the story of Jonah, wouldn't it have been strange for Jonah to present himself to the Ninevites and say, "Let my people go!" Of course, that would be ridiculous, because we would all say, "Wait a minute…didn't Moses actually say that to the Pharaoh on behalf of the Israelites?!" Yeah, I think you get the point.

Occasionally a pastor might say something that another pastor has said because they are all preaching from the same Bible and at times use the same words and cultural references of their time to illustrate the Bible—that happens sometimes. And I am not saying that a pastor cannot quote another pastor or be inspired by another pastor's sermon. Furthermore, there may be times when God tells a pastor to recycle a particular sermon because it needs to be heard again. But when a pastor perpetually refuses to pray and study to get a message from God or they just download a message from another pastor to preach, they are unfaithful. In effect, they are telling God and their congregation, "You are not worth the time and effort." Because if they actually cared and believed what they were doing was important, they would put the time into their study and spend time with God.

These are just a few examples of the unfaithfulness of the Hireling pastor. Just like Jesus is implying, these "hired" shepherds/pastors "abandon" the sheep when the wolf comes. In other words, if there is anything that threatens their own comfort level, Hirelings will run away from the responsibility of caring for God's sheep/congregation. However, I thank God that there are great pastors out there. Pastors who are actually called and are doing their best to imitate "the good shepherd (Jesus)," for their congregations.

The Hirelings Price Keeps Them Out Of God's Will

I was having a conversation with a pastor and he was in the process of looking for a new church to serve within his denomination. I asked him what was the criteria he was looking for in a potential church. He told me that the church he was serving currently could not afford him, and the next church he would pastor would need to meet his salary requirements of a minimum of $55,000 per year.

Now before I delve into my issue with his criteria I need to state that there is nothing wrong with supporting a pastor financially. People often fail to realize the amount of work a true pastor puts in. I have known pastors that have talked people out of suicide, helped brings families back together, answered phone calls of hurting people in the middle of the night, and the like. It is no stretch of the imagination to say that pastors save peoples' lives. They also deal with the pressure of realizing that one day they will stand before God for every sermon, counseling session, how they managed church funds, and the list goes on and on. A pastor never clocks out. They know that who they are privately as well as publicly will have an impact on their congregation and the community they serve. This is why the writer of Hebrews speaks so highly of Christian leaders and says, *"Have confidence in your leaders and submit to their authority, because they keep watch over you as those who must give an account,"* (Hebrews 13:17a).

Pastors do the work of counselors; they are spiritual surgeons; they are as good as, if not better than professional/motivational speakers; they save lives like a firefighter; some have great social and networking skills that are parallel to the greatest of entrepreneurs; they are life coaches who come beside you and help you in areas of leadership and more. Oftentimes they are just as available to the congregation as you would expect a 911 dispatcher to be; some have attained master's degrees in theology and pastoral care; others have great administrative and managerial skills. And yet, while they do the job of a professional counselor, a 911 dispatcher, a life coach, speaker, etc., and some having even attained degrees to benefit the people they serve, there are still those that assume a pastor should not be supported financially. In short, I personally have had pastors make sacrifices for me to be successful (you pastors in my life know who you are). There are pastors that have spent hours in prayer for me. Therefore, I personally believe a true pastor never gets paid enough. Some pastors will elect to work another job on top of their already pressured calling of being a pastor.

Nonetheless, the Bible makes provision for pastors to be supported financially (1 Timothy 5:17-18).

With the idea of pastors being supported financially out of the way, now let's discuss what was wrong with the pastor's criteria. What bothered me is that this particular pastor put a price tag on where he was willing to go to serve God because he was a Hireling. And yet, the numerous characters in the Bible never had the luxury of putting a price tag on where they would serve God. When did Moses, Elijah, Deborah, or Mary ever say, "God, I will only serve this particular people or community if the price is right." No, they never said that! They did what God called and sent them to do, and God took care of them. Regardless of how hard and daunting the task may be, the true pastor will go and serve the community to which God has called them, trusting that God will provide. For the true pastor, they believe the Red Sea will part, they believe there will be a ram in the bush, they believe God will save them from a fiery furnace. But for the Hireling pastor, they always have a price because they do not fully trust God to take care of them. So they either do the service where they get paid the most, receive the most accolades, or what is the least costly to them. While these Hireling pastors may seem to have faith, their true motivation is self-preservation and fear. Their price outweighs the calling of God.

A Real Pastor Cannot Be Fired

Hirelings just have a job, and they see it that way. Therefore, because they have a job instead of a calling from God, they can be fired. Basically, the Hireling only wants to accomplish the job description. They pray but are not really expecting God to direct them, so they just do the job and look forward to being off the clock so they can do what they really want to do. It is not always the case that the Hireling does not really care about the congregation, they are just not willing to make a sacrifice on behalf of the congregation. They were hired by a church to do a certain job, and if they don't do it, they get fired and move on to the next ministry, church, or stop pastoring altogether because it's just not worth it for them—They have a price.

However, when you think about Biblical characters like Abraham...did he have a job? Did the prophet Jeremiah have a job? What about Jesus' mother, Mary...did she have a job? No, they had a calling from God. They weren't Hirelings that only wanted to follow a job description. They could not be fired by anyone because they weren't hired by anyone. They directly followed the King of kings. And when things got tough, they could not quit like the Hireling does and look for another job. Jeremiah once felt like quitting the mission God had given him, but he said that when he tried to stop delivering God's message, then God's Word irritated him. Holding onto what God told him to speak became like a fire in his bones (Jeremiah 20:7-9). Why? Because he was called and could not quit doing that which God told him to do. Even Jesus felt like not going to the cross, but because of His calling He went to the cross for us anyway (Luke 22:39-44). Could you imagine people trying to tell the Apostle Paul, "You're fired!" No, that's hard to imagine because real pastors of God don't have a job, they have a calling. They don't do what they do because of a job description or because someone hired them. They simply follow the orders of the God that called and sent them.

I am not saying that a true pastor can't apply to a church where the pastor's position is vacant. Nor am I saying that God can't send a pastor to a church for a season and then move that pastor somewhere else—God does do that. Nonetheless, it should be God sending the pastor. Pastors should know that God is sending them to a people and/or for a season. Jonah may have been reluctant, but he knew the people to which God called him, Moses knew the people to which he was called, Paul knew he was called to the Gentiles. The true pastor goes to a people not because of price or job description but because God has ordained it. The called pastor can be disqualified by God from their call due to disobedience and/or unrepentant sin. God's anointing and blessing may be removed from a pastor that was once called. But a true pastor that is obedient to God can never be fired because they work directly for God.

Denominational, associational, or any man-made job descriptions don't apply, the real pastor knows what God sent them to do. Every congregation should want a pastor that has a calling from God and not a Hireling.

Reasons Why You Don't Spot A Hireling

The body of Christ should be able to spot a Hireling. However, the Devil is very crafty and deceiving. Hence, in the following is a list of why we are blinded to the Hireling:

Charismatic personality: Their personality is larger than life. They have a magnetism in their personality that is winsome. So their motives, theology, and morality are never questioned because you think, "This pastor is such an awesome person."

Nice: You assume that because the pastor is "nice" they must be from God. However, there are nice atheists too.

Gifted: "Well, they are so gifted." Yeah, and so was Lucifer but he became Satan. A pastor can have great spiritual gifts, communication, and administrative capabilities and still not be called by God. Remember

Satan was such a gifted communicator that he talked Adam and Eve out of the Garden.

Flattery: They tell you everything you want to hear, but not what you need to hear. They never say anything that challenges you, so you assume they are called by God. However, a true pastor will lovingly challenge you to live a life of greater admiration, obedience, and holiness towards God.

Appearance: Sadly, sometimes if the pastor is a certain skin color, height, build, or wears a certain clothing style, then our carnal assumptions make us think "This person must be from God."

These are just to name a few reasons why we can't spot the Hireling. This is not to say that a real pastor cannot have a big personality or wear a certain clothing style. It just should not be the main thing we're looking for when discerning if a pastor is of God or not. We just cannot assume anymore that all pastors are from God. We don't have to be overly hyper about it but we must remember that there are *"false apostles, deceitful workers, masquerading as apostles of Christ. And no wonder, for Satan himself masquerades as an angel of light. It is not surprising, then, if his servants also masquerade as servants of righteousness. Their end will be what their actions deserve,"* (2 Corinthians 11:13-15).

A Powerful People Not A Powerful Person

The content in this book is prophetic in nature, I know God wanted me to write this book for the entire body of Christ. The Church of Jesus Christ has been hurt and crippled by Hirelings. When the Hireling is in charge of a church, they rob the congregation of power. The focus becomes about what the Hireling wants or is comfortable with, and not what God wants for the people. Whereas the Church was supposed to be about a powerful people, the Hireling makes it about a powerful person, namely…themselves. In other words, a pastor should be equipping and strengthening a congregation, but because the Hireling has a price they consciously or unconsciously make it all about themselves.

When people think about the Exodus story, most people think about Moses. But really what Moses did is to help empower the people of God. He was not a Hireling, but as God's man he liberated and strengthened God's people as any real pastor would do. Hence, when I read the Exodus story I see powerful people, not just a powerful person. Look again at the story and see for yourself:

"The Egyptians urged the people to hurry and leave the country. 'For otherwise,' they said, 'we will all die!' So the

people took their dough before the yeast was added, and carried it on their shoulders in kneading troughs wrapped in clothing. The Israelites did as Moses instructed and asked the Egyptians for articles of silver and gold and for clothing. The Lord had made the Egyptians favorably disposed toward the people, and they gave them what they asked for; so they plundered the Egyptians." (Exodus 12:33-36)

Did the text say the Egyptians feared for their lives because of Moses? No, the Egyptians were so afraid of losing their lives because of all the powerful demonstrations of Israel's God, that they asked the Israelites to leave—they were afraid of the Israelite people. Moreover, the Israelites did not leave Egypt without first plundering their gold, silver, and clothing. Yes, Moses was a powerful man, but what we see in the text is a powerful people! The Hireling makes it about themselves, whereas the called pastor of God, the real pastor of God, empowers the people they are sent to.

My prayer is that this book would return the power back to the Church (the people of God). This is not to say that we don't need called men and women of God in the Church for leadership. God has given us different types of church leaders (apostles, prophets, evangelists, pastors, and teachers) to equip the Church. However, many Hirelings have hijacked these ministerial titles/gifts without having a true call from God, and therefore, have become ineffective or even damaging to the body of Christ

While I will continue to speak boldly about this subject, it is important to remember as stated earlier that in using our discernment, it is for the sake of the truth, love, and the redemption of people. I believe that God is in the redemption business, and I am hoping that should a pastor who has a shattered pulpit read this book, that they would repent and be restored. Not every pastor knows they have a shattered pulpit, because they may have been taught to do ministry with a Hireling mentality. They have led and done ministry in ignorance, but hopefully, this will be a turning point for them. This book is also for every Christian who has been waiting for a book like this. Who has been sensing that many pulpits in America and the world, have been shattered by Hirelings. This book will affirm what you have sensed but perhaps never had the courage or words to express. I believe this book will bring healing to the body Christ. In the next few chapters, we will unapologetically break down the many Hirelings behind shattered pulpits. Buckle up and let's go!

TWO

WOLF IN SHEEP'S CLOTHING PASTOR

Jesus made an interesting statement in Matthew 7:15: *"Watch out for false prophets. They come to you in sheep's clothing, but inwardly they are ferocious wolves."* While every Hireling is dangerous and even lethal to the body of Christ, this one is the most vicious. They are indeed messengers of Satan who have crept into pulpits with people being unaware. This Hireling is to be considered as dangerous as a militant terrorist. Why are they a wolf in sheep's clothing? Because they have every intention of eating the sheep!

This Hireling believes the congregation exists for their own selfish ambitions and not for God. They believe the congregation is for their own consumption. So the house of God becomes a place of business, instead of an environment in which God is glorified and His people are edified. They turn God's house into a whore house where they prostitute God's people for their own personal gain. Jesus had an encounter like this where He appeared to what was supposed to be a house of prayer, but it was turned into a business. Jesus was so furious with these

Hirelings turning God's house into a marketplace that He started flipping over the tables, scattered their money on the floor, made a whip, and chased people out of the temple (John 2:14-16). Jesus was righteously angry because He knew these wolves in sheep's clothing were violently undermining God's people.

It needs to be said before going further that prosperity is not a bad thing. We should not assume that having an abundance of money, being able to go on vacations, and enjoying life is a problem. God does get enjoyment when we enjoy His creation within the proper boundaries. If God has given us gifts such as laughter, the taste of good food, and even sexual intimacy within the safety of a godly marriage, then He must be a good God who enjoys watching His creation find pleasure in His gifts. But as it has been said before…if we love the gifts, more than we love the Gift Giver (which is this Hireling's downfall), then that's a problem. It is not a problem to have money and possessions, but it is a problem if money and possessions have you! Remember, God was happy to bless David with wealth. David not only enjoyed the prosperity for himself, but he passed it onto his son, Solomon, to build a beautiful temple for God (1 Chronicles 29:1-5). It pleased God to give wealth to Isaac because everywhere Isaac went he built altars for God (Genesis 26:12-14). Money is just a tool we can use as Christians to enjoy and overthrow the kingdom of darkness. Imagine God blessing you with finances to where you could leave an inheritance for your family (Proverbs 13:22), pay for people's education, feed the homeless, build orphanages, etc. Money is only a problem when it is in the wrong hands.

These Hirelings are hedonistic. Meaning that the idea of self-gratification or pleasure is always on their mind. They view the congregation as piggy banks, groupies, customers and unfortunately in some cases, sex objects for their own pleasure. They are indeed wolves in sheep's clothing, taking advantage of the Lord's people.

Manipulates People

I will never forget having a disturbing conversation I had with a future pastor during my time in seminary. I knew this person had struggled with some sexual sin but I didn't know how deep the problem was until we had a conversation about ministry. He told me that when he had finished seminary and was leading a church, he was going to tell women in pre-marital counseling that it was important for a wife to perform fellatio on her husband. This fellow student literally told me that he would urge women to perform oral sex on a regular basis for their husband if they wanted to have a steady marriage. He did not mention anything about God, love, trust, respect, or transparency as a part of a healthy marriage, he just claimed that fellatio was the most important thing.

Where is this in the Bible? Where in the Bible does it say that a woman has to perform fellatio? The answer is…it's not in there. So in the future event in which he would be counseling a woman, who is about to be married, he would impose his own sexual desires on the bride to be. He would manipulate her into believing that, "In order to be a good wife I must perform fellatio." After hearing his views on premarital counseling, I strongly rebuked him never to say anything like that. What is interesting is that he was a phenomenal preacher. He was a great communicator in the pulpit, and because of that skill many people didn't recognize he was the "Wolf In Sheep's Clothing Pastor." Unfortunately, he graduated from seminary and as far as I know is currently pastoring a church. I pray for the sake of his congregation that he has been changed by the grace of God.

This isn't the only sexual vice I have encountered or heard about with these Hirelings. One time I was doing evangelism in my neighborhood. I was checking on people to see if they needed prayer and inviting them to our church. I was invited into a home and the lady of the house told me that she used to participate in a church until she had a problem with the pastor that was counseling her. Basically, several years ago she was thinking about getting a divorce from her husband. She met with the pastor a couple of times privately for counseling. This pastor told her that while she was having troubles with her husband it was okay to have relations with other men. And in particular, this pastor hinted and tried to manipulate her into a sexual relationship with himself. She refused the pastor's advancements and unfortunately still got a divorce from her husband. So here was a woman, who needed real godly counsel and instead she got a perverted Hireling who was the "Wolf In Sheep's Clothing Pastor." I told this lady I was sorry she had that issue, and how real pastors would never want to dishonor God or God's people with that type of behavior.

Beyond sexual deviance, I remember witnessing a pastor urging a congregation to give money. As alluded to earlier there is nothing wrong with believing God for prosperity in your life. The widow at Zarephath was promised by God through the prophet Elijah that if she gave some of her last meal to the prophet during a drought/famine, she would never run out of food again for the duration of the drought/ famine (1 Kings 17:7-16). However, this pastor's whole notion for giving was about giving for personal rewards. What about giving to advance the Gospel? What about giving because it's worship to God? Certainly, God can reward you for your giving (Malachi 3:10, Luke 6:38). Nonetheless, the motivation of our giving should not be to put God in our debt so that He has to owe us. No, God acts according to His Word and His will, not because we believe He owes us. We give cheerfully to the work and mission of God because we are grateful for what God has done. And yes, because God is a loving and gracious God He does bless us in a multiplicity of ways for our giving. The point being is this: Are we giving because we love God or because we just want God to owe us?

It appeared like this pastor wanted to make God out to be a vending machine in which you could use your faith as currency, and God would give you whatever you wanted. He was so forceful in his plea to get people to give that he ended up doing something inexcusable. He stepped into the crowd, reached into a woman's purse, pulled out some money, and threw it into the offering plate. Everybody began to shout and got excited about what the pastor had done. Even the woman whose purse was broken into didn't seem to have a problem with it. The woman should have been able to make a cheerful decision to give in faith. However, the pastor circumvented that idea, taking away any faith decision on her part. When I saw this I didn't think this was a faithful pastor, I only thought of a manipulating bully behind the pulpit—his pulpit was indeed shattered. What great manipulators these Hirelings are!

Uses People

I am the Pastor of an awesome church called Well of Life, in Hammond, Louisiana. I know it's expected of me to say my church is awesome, but I'm telling the truth—it really is awesome. Our church was established on September 4th, 2016. Before we established ourselves as a new church, I spent a lot of time praying for and meeting people that might be called to help launch the church. I remember sitting down at a coffee shop with someone who expressed an interest in joining the worship team. I talked with the guy for a while and gave him some of the vision for our church. I assumed since he responded to one of the flyers about starting a new church, and because he wanted to be on the worship team that he must have been a Christian. But somewhere in the conversation, when I asked him about his relationship with Christ, he said, "I don't really care that much about God and I have a problem with Christians."

He went on to say, "I'm good at the drums and I would love to join your worship team." In response, I said, "Didn't you hear what I said earlier?" "Whatcha mean?" he replied. "Earlier in the conversation, I told you how our church is committed to not using people, because you have a problem with God and Christians, why don't we have a few more conversations over a cup of coffee, you can come to some of our Bible studies, and then at a certain point if you feel closer to God and start liking Christians, we will talk about you joining the worship team."

The reason why I denied his request to join the worship team is that I cared more about the state of his spirit than his talent. He needed to know that I cared more about him having a relationship with God than using him for his talent. If I had put him on the worship team he would have seen it as a hobby or a performance, instead of actually leading the people into a deeper admiration of God. He would have viewed the congregation as his fans, instead of helping disciples be closer to Christ through music.

The Hireling pastor, however, would have absolutely used this musician. They would have put him on the worship team knowing that he didn't have a relationship with Christ, and thus supporting his lack of respect and admiration for God. Or sometimes the Hireling thinks, "Well, I know he doesn't have a relationship with Christ, but I'll put him or her on the worship team because we need a drummer, and then hopefully in the process, he or she will become a Christian." While it seems like a logical move, it shows little care for the unsaved person. The pastor is dealing with serious matters of life and death, Heaven or Hell, we should not be gambling with people's lives, using them for their talents and not taking the time to care for their spiritual condition.

The reason the Hireling uses people is that the Hireling needs them. The Hireling "needs" people to feel validated for their ministry. They need people for their own self-absorbed reasons—this Hireling is needy. However, the true pastor has wants and desires for people. They want to see people come to know Jesus Christ. They want people to grow more in the sanctification process. They want people to pursue their God-given calling. Because the true pastor "wants" they inspire and support, but because the Hireling "needs" they manipulate and take. The true pastor will never use people to feel validated, they already feel validated by God.

Shallow By Nature

This type of Hireling does everything in their power to avoid any discomfort and persuades their congregation to do the same. Therefore, their church services have a tendency to be shallow. They never preach anything that would challenge the congregation to live a more prudent life. And if they come close to the idea of God placing demands on the congregation's lives, they will sugar coat it by talking primarily about the blessings for obedience and mentioning little to nothing about the consequences of disobedience. They only talk about the things the congregation already supports and approves. If the congregation is more liberal, conservative, of a certain ethnicity, or culture this Hireling only preaches toward those aims to be pleasing to the congregation but not to be pleasing to God. Because after all, they don't want people to be upset by the truth and leave, that would have a negative impact on the offering and their agenda.

This Hireling is more focused on performance than allowing the Holy Spirit to control the ministry. The coffee has to be perfect, the music has to be perfect, the sermon needs to have many popular culture references in order to be relevant. Everybody on stage needs to be flawless looking, the children's programs just need to be fun— it doesn't need solid teaching. The congregation is treated more like a customer or a client instead of a disciple of Christ. In everything they do, they try to portray a faith that is always easy, relaxed, fun and is without moments of pain, suffering, and serious questions that impact our lives. This Hireling simply attempts to numb people from their pain through entertainment or whimsical thoughts, without discussing or dealing with the harsh tangible struggles of life.

However, the book of Psalms' presentation of faith isn't so serialized, pretty, neat, and clean. The writers of the Psalms expressed great faith and joy, but also great pain and discomfort. But these Hirelings would have you believe that if you are always healthy and wealthy, you must have great faith. But what about Jesus? He had the ultimate faith, He was perfect, and yet, He experienced an incomprehensible level of pain for our sins. Even Job who was a righteous man was wealthy and had great faith, but

Job also went through a very tough season of his life. And what I love about Job is that he accepted both the good and bad that God allowed into his life. So much so that when he lost his possessions and his children he said, *"'Naked I came from my mother's womb, and naked I will depart. The Lord gave and the Lord has taken away; May the name of the Lord be praised,'"* (Job 1:21).

While God does prosper us, He will at times allow us to go through hardships to strengthen our faith. Abraham had to deal with a famine; Daniel had to go into the lion's Den; David faced a giant; John the Baptist was beheaded; and Jesus faced a cross. We also live in a world that is hostile or contrary to the things of God (Romans 8:7), so of course, we will have enemies in this life. Jesus even told us that because He was persecuted, His followers would be too (John15:20). Just like Job, the true Christian understands that in this life, money comes and goes, people come and go, comfort comes and goes, but God is always there. While a person without Christ feels like all that they have are their material goods and people, and they are lost without them; the believer knows that even without those possessions and people, God still cares for them and there is a greater reward to be attained while on earth and the life that is to come.

For the sake of clarity, it needs to be said that just because a church has a coffee shop, uses cultural references, or has flashing lights during the service, doesn't inherently mean the church or its pastor is ungodly. It is only when these things become the means of evangelism and replace the Gospel that it is a problem. Nonetheless, these Hirelings do a disservice to the body of Christ by always presenting a shallow faith that seems to be devoid of any real obstacles. They make people believe that if they have any struggles at all, then they must not be faithful Christians. This is simply a false dichotomy. The Bible makes it clear that there is a real struggle to overcome in this life (Ephesians 6:12, Matthew 24:13). Christians need the power of the Gospel, the Holy Spirit, and other believers to encourage them; they don't just need to be entertained.

They Want To Be An Idol

I was talking over the phone with a friend of mine, and we were talking about different ministries and their impact. And then my friend brought up an interesting thought. He mentioned two prominent pastors in our culture today. If I said their names you would know them. So for the sake of confidentially, let's reference to these ministers as "Pastor A" and "Pastor B". My friend said, "When you think about Pastor A what comes to mind?" I said, "I think about the multiple campuses, the amazing preaching, the vibrant worship team, their model of ministry, and how relatable they are!" My friend replied, "Okay...so when I mention Pastor B what comes to mind?" I said, "I think about God, and how we should be closer to Him. How we need to lose our pride and really submit our lives to Christ. Pastor B is really serious about connecting us to God." In response, my friend laughed and said, "Brian, notice that when you talked about Pastor A, you talked about his ministry and all the things he was doing…you didn't mention God because you were focused on Pastor A. But when you talked about Pastor B, you mentioned God and how we should be responding to God!" He then went on to say, "Pastor A makes it about himself and a person's faith will rise or fall based on what Pastor A does. Pastor B makes it about God, and that's where our faith should really be."

Pastor A represents the Hireling that is the "Wolf In Sheep's Clothing Pastor." They make it all about themselves. While they would never admit it, this Hireling is interested in turning the congregation into their fans instead of disciples. They would love for the congregation to turn them into an idol, worshipping this pastor instead of the Lord. This is not to say that you cannot be inspired by pastors—of course, you can. God will even direct your steps to connect with certain pastors/Christian leaders that you can trust to help you on your faith journey. If we can honor police officers, firefighters, presidents, and military personnel, then we should be willing to honor the pastors that watch after our souls. But we are by no means to turn them into idols; yet, this is what happens! And quite frankly I'm tired of it, and so is God.

The Apostle Paul dealt with a situation where people were clamoring over preachers instead of the Lord (1 Corinthians 1:10-17). He admonished them to stop turning preachers into idols and to put their focus on Christ. I admonished you, the reader, in the same way. You are not cattle, you are not groupies or fans, you are disciples of the Lord Jesus Christ, you are loved by God! Do not allow yourselves to be used and consumed by the "Wolf In Sheep's Clothing Pastor," be inspired by godly people but please, don't turn them into idols. Beware, just because it looks like a sheep, does not mean it is a sheep. It could be a wolf with really sharp teeth.

Solving The Problem

(This section will be at the end of every chapter to remind you of this truth.)

Dear reader, it's important for you to know that the "Wolf In Sheep's Clothing Pastor" and the other pastors/Hirelings mentioned in this book can absolutely be restored! God loves all people, including the pastors who might have lost their way. If you are a Christian leader and you feel convicted as you are reading the contents of this book, then you need to know that conviction doesn't mean condemnation (Romans 8:1). God loves you and is using this book as a wake-up call for you to turn some things around.

Therefore, while this book has/will diagnose the many problems behind the pulpit, let's not write these pastors off too quickly. God has provided a way for pastors to be restored. In chapter ten, I will reveal the solution for this pervasive problem in a section entitled, "Problem Solved." Because of Christ, there is hope.

THREE

SOCIAL JUSTICE PASTOR

Jesus and His disciples were once staying in the home of some friends in a town called Bethany. The hosts prepared a meal in honor of Jesus. One of the hosts, Mary (not the Virgin Mary), poured an expensive perfume on the feet of Jesus as an act of worship. And the disciple known as Judas got upset. He believed it was a bad use of the perfume and that they could have sold the perfume and used the money for the poor. But Jesus rejected his objection. In essence, Jesus told Judas that there will always be poor people, and what Mary did was just as or even more important than taking care of the poor (John 12:1-8).

The Hireling known as the "Social Justice Pastor" is very much like Judas in this passage. Aside from the fact that Judas was a money hungry thief, this particular Hireling is so focused on the poor (social justice issues) that they totally miss or overlook Jesus! Just like Judas they are constantly saying, "Let's take care of the poor" or "Let's take care of a social issue." Thus, they think and persuade their congregation that the pinnacle of spiritual maturity is pursuing social justice. For the sake of clarity, I must say that we are to do social justice. God's Word compels us to do so (James 1:27, Proverbs 28:27, Micah 6:8). But when our devotion to doing social justice becomes greater than our devotion to God that's a problem. This is why Jesus rebuked Judas so strongly, and exalted Mary for blessing Him with rich perfume—Because Mary's devotion to Christ was second to nothing else, not even social justice issues. To paraphrase what Jesus was saying to Judas, it was as if He said, "There will always be social justice issues to deal with in a sinful, imperfect world, so don't forget about your devotion to me," (John 12:7-8).

Some of you still might be gasping for air while reading this section because you are thinking, "So...is he saying the pursuit of social justice is a bad thing?" And my answer is "NO," of course social justice is a noble pursuit, but it should not become an idol. Imagine for a moment a man that is a workaholic. He spends hours at work, getting the job done, changing people's lives, making a great salary, but he never spends any time with his wife and children. His wife complains to him saying, "When are you going to make time for us?" In response, he says, "We live in a great house that's in a great neighborhood, we can go on vacations multiple times a year, our kids have the best education, my work has helped a lot of people, and has allowed me to make our lives and the lives of others better, we lack for nothing...so please don't complain about my work hours." And then the wife says, "But your children miss you, I miss you, we are lacking your devotion towards us." You may do a lot of great social justice exploits and change the world, but if you forget your God, as the example of this husband forgetting his family, that is not right and you have missed what Christianity is about.

Hopefully, the problem is becoming clearer for you now. The sin of this Hireling that is a "Social Justice Pastor" is that they whore themselves or are available for every single social justice concern, but they forget to have a strong devotion to Christ. They feel like they are accomplishing so much when they ridicule governments that are oppressing people or they place a bumper sticker on their car that opposes a certain idea. Sometimes this type of Hireling is not doing much financially or physically to ease the suffering of the world, but they certainly want you to think they are by constantly posting comments online or talking about the issues. Their mouths are forever expressing the issues but they are not willing to make sacrifices to make things better. They manipulate almost every scripture towards some type of social injustice. Their biggest and most blasphemous problem is that they act as if salvation can be found in the pursuit of social justice when it can only be found in Christ.

And while issues of inequality, bigotry, sexual misconduct, nature, and the like are important issues in the mind of God, they are not the main issues. The reason there are social injustices of various forms is because of sin. But this type of Hireling doesn't see it that way. They are always blaming the problem on a big institution, political parties, conservatives, liberals, and ignorance. They are always responding to the symptoms of the problem instead of the root of the issue. For them, it is not that people are evil, it is the idea of capitalism, socialism, government, class, and educational systems that are to be blamed. They assume that if you got rid of some of these ideas or institutions then human suffering would cease. However, what they fail to realize is that these broken systems are just a reflection of the brokenness in humanity.

Ignores Sin In The Guise Of Social Justice

This type of Hireling doesn't put a major emphasis on personal sin. It's almost as if they want people to believe that human beings aren't so bad, they just have bad ideas. However, where do these bad ideas originate from? We have these bad ideas, philosophies, murders, rapes, and so on, because people produce them. This Hireling really believes people can be educated away from their sin. But according to the Bible, we must be "born again" (John 3:7). It is not just a matter of behavioral modification or education as this Hireling might lead one to believe. Instead, a person must be saved by Jesus Christ thus becoming a Christian that is forming spiritual practices, thought patterns, and habits that are reflective of Jesus Christ.

While this Hireling may every once in a while hint softly at personal sin while preaching and counseling, this Hireling doesn't really think that's the problem. And yet, Jesus thought it was such a problem that He died on the cross. Did Jesus heal the sick? Did He take care of the homeless? Was He kind to the stranger? Did Jesus do social justice? The answer to all of these questions is an overwhelming "YES." He challenged the conventional wisdom of His day; He was a political threat; He confounded the wise and humbled the powerful; He stood up for the oppressed, marginalized, and forgotten—Jesus is AMAZING and nobody understands or performs social justice better than Jesus. But what did Jesus actually come to earth to do? He says it loud and clear: "For the Son of Man came to seek and to save the lost," (Luke 19:10). Jesus came to save sinners like you and me! He came to transform us from sinners into children of God. He pleased God the Father by living the perfect life we couldn't live, taking the punishment of sin because we couldn't handle it, resurrecting from the dead, and ascending back to the Father. I'm getting excited as I'm writing this because this is the Gospel (which means good news).

We were separated from God because of our sins, and were destined to spend eternity away from God! Why? Because a perfect God can only accept that which is perfect, and unfortunately we were tainted by sin. But because of what Jesus perfectly did on behalf of imperfect people, we now can stand before God as His children. The price of sin was too much for you or me to pay, so Christ did it for us. This is the good news known as the Christian Gospel. When Christ saves you because you accept what He did for you, then you are freed from the penalty of sin, you become free to pursue a great relationship with Christ. And yes, you will do some social justice…but you will now have a devotion to God in a way you've never had before.

These Hirelings ignore sin because they think the Gospel or salvation is about doing as much social justice as possible, and they consciously or subconsciously exemplify this to the congregation. Because the Hireling doesn't really understand the nature of the Gospel, the congregation doesn't understand how to be freed from their sin, because the Hireling acts like their sin doesn't exist. Hence, the congregation stays shackled to their demons of addiction, brokenness, and shame. The good news/Gospel is not that we get to do a whole bunch of good things, it is that we avoid the judgement of a Holy God and get to have a relationship with a merciful, loving, and righteous God along with His people. We can be relieved of our guilt and shame, and not just act like everything is okay when it's not.

Guilt Remains Because Sin Is Ignored

Imagine going to the doctor's office because you know that you are having stomach pains. You go over and over again, and four different times the doctor told you not to worry about it. The doctor says, "It's just in your mind… you need to relax more, eat healthier, maybe read, go for walks, and you'll feel better." You do all of these wonderful things the doctor suggests, but you still feel terrible. You visit the doctor again, and finally, he tells you that you have a terrible stomach ulcer. To your surprise, the doctor reveals that he knew since the first visit, he just didn't want to bother you with it!

Wouldn't you be upset to discover that the doctor knew what was wrong with you the entire time, and did nothing to change it? Wouldn't you be angry to know that the only reason you dealt with the pain for so long is that the doctor didn't tell you what was wrong? Now as ridiculous as this fictional story is, this is exactly what the "Social Justice Pastor" does.

Once again this Hireling doesn't want to deal with your sin, so they just get the congregation to focus on social justice. Meanwhile, some members in the congregation have some real guilt and shame that could be alleviated with the power of the Gospel, but the Hireling doesn't share it, possibly because the Hireling doesn't know the Gospel, and cannot administer what the Hireling has not received.

I have learned from doing ministry for quite some time now that it's not talking about Hell that deters people from God. It's not talking about living a moral life. It's not even talking about tithing or being more accountable to a local church (I understand there might be exceptions). However, I have discovered that what deters people from God the most, is that people don't want to admit they are as bad as they really are and that they need forgiveness. People want to believe it's always somebody else's fault: "It's what my parents didn't do; it's what the government does; it's what "them" or "they" did. It's certainly not me…I'm always the victim!" And yes, at times there can be other people or entities to blame. But the reality is all people have sinned and are in need of forgiveness (Romans 3:23). Nonetheless, this Hireling helps enforce this victim mentality, and that people are naturally good and we just need more education and social justice, but what we all really need is salvation.

Some people know they have sinned and want to be set free. Have you ever needed to vent? Have you ever had a concern or you did something wrong and needed someone to talk to? How painful would it be to hold onto guilt and shame and not be able to get relief? Nonetheless, this Hireling does the congregation a disservice as they are looking for a place to dump their guilt and shame. And yet, this Hireling ignores their sin, tells them they are good people because they care about whales, the environment, and the poor. But, no matter how much social justice they pursue, in their heart they know they have sinned and need forgiveness.

So let me say what the "Social Justice Pastor" won't say: Your sin was so heinous, grotesque, nasty, disturbing, perverted, and demonic that Jesus died for your sins, however, you were also so precious, beautiful, wonderful, and delightful to God that Jesus died for your sins! Thanks be to God, you were guilty of sin and destined for Hell; but because of God's great love for you, because of what Christ has done, you are set free from guilt, shame, and Hell, if you are willing to accept the free gift of salvation.

They Don't Believe In The Devil

Because this Hireling doesn't have a real notion of personal sin that must be confessed and a heart that must be repentant, they also don't really believe there is a Devil. If they do believe in a type of devil, it's just the ideas and institutions they feel are holding people back. But the Bible speaks about an actual Devil and demonic forces that

Christians are to stand their ground against in Jesus name (1 Peter 5:8, Ephesians 6:10-17).

When I was in seminary, I remember one of my fellow students telling me how he struggled to listen to my comments in class because he didn't like when I brought up the tough parts of the Bible. He said that he preferred me to not talk about God's wrath, Hell, or the Devil. What is interesting is that these subjects are clearly in the Bible, and I do talk a lot about the love, grace, and mercy of God, it's just that I don't ignore the parts of the Bible that make people uncomfortable either. So if you're thinking, "Why would someone in seminary, studying to be a pastor, not want to talk about serious matters, such as wrath, Hell, and the Devil?" Because again, this type of Hireling doesn't want to believe the Devil exists or any other tough parts of the Scripture that would suggest there is a Devil or that God has wrath. If you are serious about the Bible, it's hard to learn anything Scriptural from the "Social Justice Pastor," because they only want to talk about the pleasant parts of the Scripture. You don't have to take pastors like this too seriously, because they certainly don't take themselves seriously. They look to turn every subject into social justice issues, in which they believe we will all be saved if we just have more compassion, joy, and love. While social justice is a part of the Christian life, it is not the Gospel.

Their Greatest Desire Is For World Peace

World peace is a good thing. We should all want world peace. However, the true pastor understands that if there is going to be world peace, it's going to be because people submit to the Lord Jesus Christ (Philippians 2:10-11). The fact of the matter is, until Jesus returns, there will not be world peace because not everyone wants to follow Jesus. If Jesus is both Savior and Lord, if He is the Creator of the world, if He is God, and these are all things Scripture claims about Jesus; and yet, there are people who don't want to submit to Him, how can there be world peace? When there are people claiming that it is their choice to open up strip clubs; it is their choice to worship other gods (which are just demons in disguise); when they blaspheme the name God; all of these are things the Christian Bible speaks against, how will there be world peace in the midst of all of this? I know there would be peace and love in the world if everybody actually wanted to give their life to Jesus Christ—because God is love (1 John 4:7-21). But that is not the case.

Even Jesus mentioned how His presence would cause division:

"'Do not suppose that I have come to bring peace to the earth. I did not come to bring peace, but a sword. For I have come to turn a man against his father, a daughter against her mother, a daughter-in-law against her mother-in-law—a man's enemies will be the members of his own household. I've come to bring a sword.'" (Matthew 10:34-36)

Jesus is stating that the root cause of division is that people will vary in their acceptance of Him. Basically, these Hirelings think you can have world peace without Christ. They really believe that the greatest enemies are the institutions and philosophies of the world, and if we can just remove those institutions and give people positive thoughts, then there will be world peace. But the reality is, any notion of world peace without the Creator, is a falsehood and will never be sustainable. Now the believer can have peace in a sinful world because of the Holy Spirit indwelling the Christian (Isaiah 26:3, Galatians 5:22). Nevertheless, for there to be peace in the world, where there is no more war, manipulation, depression, and so on, then we must submit to Christ. And unfortunately, the entire world is not going to do that. But one day, Jesus will separate the Christians from non-Christians, saved and unsaved, and there will be peace for those that have submitted to the Lordship of Jesus Christ (Revelation 21:1-5). But this is not what the Hireling preaches although it is Biblically sound.

Social Justice Is A Must, But It Must Not Replace The Christ

While I have mentioned the importance of social justice some, I want to make it explicitly clear here: Social justice is a good thing and even Jesus gave the disciples a picture of how social justice plays a role when He returns to the earth:

"When the Son of Man comes in his glory, and all the angels with him, he will sit on his glorious throne. All the nations will be gathered before him, and he will separate the people one from another as a shepherd separates the sheep from the goats. He will put the sheep on his right and the goats on his left. Then the King will say to those on his right, 'Come, you who are blessed by my Father; take your inheritance, the kingdom prepared for you since the creation of the world. For I was hungry and you gave me something to eat, I was thirsty and you gave me something to drink, I was a stranger and you invited me in, I needed clothes and you clothed me, I was sick and you looked after me, I was in prison and you came to visit me.' 'Then the righteous will answer him, 'Lord, when did we see you hungry and feed you, or thirsty and give you something to drink? When did we see you a stranger and invite you in, or needing clothes and clothe you? When did we see you

sick or in prison and go to visit you?' 'The King will reply, 'Truly I tell you, whatever you did for one of the least of these brothers and sisters of mine, you did for me.'" (Luke 25:31-40)

I love this picture that Jesus paints of the coming Kingdom. He acknowledges His disciples for their acts of social justice. That the good we have done for other people will be as if we did it for Jesus. But it's not their works of social justice that saves them, it's their relationship with Christ. Of course, disciples do acts of social justice because we are imitating the Savior. But we also know it's not our works that save us but the grace of God (Ephesians 2:8-9).

The point I'm trying to make is that what ultimately matters is our devotion to Christ. Do you have a prayer life? Do you have a desire for God's Word? Do you find yourself thinking about Christ? Because real Christians do. While we should pursue acts of social justice, they should flow out of our prayer life, out of our pursuit of Christ, out of our love for Christ. So don't forget to practice justice, but you must not forget Christ.

Think about the thieves on the crosses next to Jesus. One thief mocked Jesus but the other found devotion towards Jesus. One thief in the midst of suffering for his crimes recognized that Jesus was suffering and was innocent. He recognized that in Christ was salvation. So, that one thief fixed his heart and mind on Christ and asked Him to be saved. And Jesus promised him that on the very same day of his death he would be in "paradise" with Him (Luke 23:39-43). Now, what did that thief do to deserve Heaven? He wasn't even a Christian very long, he just converted when he was about to die! He didn't do any great acts of social justice. But he did put his trust in Jesus Christ. In his moment of weakness, he did develop a devotion for Christ, and that was enough.

Please, dear Christian, do social justice. But just remember that we have all these social issues because of the Fall in the Garden of Eden. Before sin was introduced to the world through Adam's sin, humanity lived in harmony with God. Therefore, since our primary purpose is to be in relationship with God, let's not make a product of the Fall (all these sinful social injustices) the main thing. Christ is the main thing! Ever since Christ died, rose, and ascended back to Heaven, we can now have a vibrant relationship with God—pursue God with your heart, you won't be disappointed. He is so worthy. And be careful, because the Hireling behind a shattered pulpit—that is hyper for social justice, will have you tired chasing every social issue in the world but not Jesus.

Solving The Problem

(This section will be at the end of every chapter to remind you of this truth.)

Dear reader, it's important for you to know that the "Social Justice Pastor" and the other pastors/Hirelings mentioned in this book can absolutely be restored! God loves all people, including the pastors who might have lost their way. If you are a Christian leader and you feel convicted as you are reading the contents of this book, then you need to know that conviction doesn't mean condemnation (Romans 8:1). God loves you and is using this book as a wake-up call for you to turn some things around.

Therefore, while this book has/will diagnose the many problems behind the pulpit, let's not write these pastors off too quickly. God has provided a way for pastors to be restored. In chapter ten, I will reveal the solution for this pervasive problem in a section entitled, "Problem Solved." Because of Christ, there is hope.

FOUR

DENOMINATIONAL SERVANT PASTOR

Sometimes when I tell my salvation story I tell people I got saved at a Pentecostal church and that is how I grew up. But now that I've gotten older, I've realized that I may have been saved at a Pentecostal church, but that is not my identity. Yes, I am grateful for my upbringing in the Pentecostal church, I learned a lot about the Holy Spirit, holiness, and prayer. God was in it, and He changed my life. At another point in my life, I eventually became a Presbyterian, and I learned a great deal about having a scholarly and intellectual approach to God. God was also involved in this experience. And now I am the pastor of a church that is not a part of a denomination nor is it non-denominational, and although at first glance one might think we are like the evangelical non-denominational churches they have experienced in the past, we are nothing like that at all. People come to realize—once they connect with our church—that we are a "Kingdom church." I will explain what it means to be Kingdom later in chapter nine, but in short, a Kingdom-minded church is more than any church denomination or association one can think of. A Kingdom church seeks to establish the Kingdom of God on earth. This type of church esteems both intelligence and the supernatural workings of God. This type of church takes very seriously the idea of God's Kingdom being established on earth as it is in Heaven. It believes through grace, prayer, intelligence, and the Spirit's power that communities can truly be changed. It's the type of church that knows when to celebrate, but also knows when it's time for spiritual warfare.

Basically, Jesus didn't die so that I could become a better Pentecostal, Presbyterian, Methodist, Episcopalian, Baptist, Methodist, Lutheran, or Catholic. No, Christ died so that I could have a robust, full relationship with God and the people of God. I am a Christian! I am a Kingdom citizen! I am an ambassador of Christ! I am a child of God! And as such, I believe in the full counsel of Scripture from an intellectual and supernatural understanding. There is nothing wrong with being grateful for whatever denomination that has nurtured your faith, perhaps God was in it. However, there are a lot of things that come from denominations that are not from God. For example, there are some branches of Pentecostalism that believe speaking in tongues is required as evidence of salvation. That is simply not true. The thief on the cross who was about to die never spoke in tongues, and yet Jesus promised He would enter the Heavenly Kingdom that day (Luke 23:43). Furthermore, there are branches of Baptists that don't believe in tongues or any supernatural workings of the

Holy Spirit, aside from salvation. This too is not a right understanding. God's supernatural power works today just like we see in the Scripture. God is a good God, and I have seen Him perform the miraculous. If we believe that a dead man rose from the grave, then why do we struggle to believe in miracles today? Because regardless of what theological truth is being presented, even if it is completely Biblical, some people have been taught to have a limited view of God through their denominations.

Denominations tend to exalt one or more Biblical truths over others. Or some eliminate certain truths from the Bible completely. They galvanize their people to have a limited view of Scripture and Christian practice as well. It's just like the reasons you hang out with your friends. Ideally, the people you share friendship with have some of the same ideas, morals, and values as you. Smokers and drinkers typically mingle with smokers and drinkers, parents typically make friends with other parents, sports enthusiasts tend to fellowship with other sports enthusiasts. Moreover, some people only fellowship with people that share the same skin color, heritage, etc. It's human nature to want to be comfortable, so we make friendships with people that we share things in common with. But if you really want to learn and develop new habits, you need to extend your friendship beyond what makes you comfortable.

This is the state of denominations. They are only comfortable with the Scripture they like, the practices they like, and the people that have just as limited of a view of God and the Scripture as the denomination. Therefore, this Hireling reinforces all the ideas of the denomination. Hence, the congregation gets better at reflecting their denomination instead of the Kingdom of God. Members are taught to identify themselves more by a denominational title than as a child of God. So when you ask them if they are a Christian? They reply, "I'm a Baptist" or "I'm Catholic" or "I'm Methodist." They might not really know what their denominational title means, they just bring up how their entire family grew up in a said denomination. And what I am often tempted to say to these people is, "Your denomination didn't save you, it was Christ." If you have more affection for your denomination than you do for Christ, then you have a problem. Sometimes the congregation cannot see Christ, because the "Denominational Servant Pastor" keeps them focused more on the denomination.

They Are Puppets

These Hirelings view themselves as enlightened, inspired, and creative. Their claim to fame is that they love their congregation. And they probably do. But they stifle the congregation's growth towards Christ and the Kingdom of God because they are always thinking, "What's good for the denomination?" instead of, "What's good for the Kingdom of God?" These Hirelings are like Pinocchio, who has dreams of one day being a real boy! They have dreams of doing great things for God, dreams of being able to discern and follow the Holy Spirit, and dreams of being true leaders for their respective congregations, but they are tied down by the strings of the denomination. Whereby the higher-ups are controlling them like a puppet. Indeed the denomination is the puppeteer and their pastors are their puppets. The denomination is the ventriloquist, who is controlling the thoughts and words of their Hireling.

These Hirelings even know at times that their prayer life, spiritual wisdom, and sense of morality is greater than the puppeteers controlling them. These Hirelings could have great things to say, the Holy Spirit is trying to lead them, but they can't overcome the voice of the higher-ups controlling them. For example, within many denominations, there is a debate about who is or is not qualified for ordained ministry. These issues surround the LGBTQ community, morality, ethics, etc. And some of these denominational Hirelings believe that their denominations are making unbiblical decisions concerning who is allowed to be ordained or not, especially over whether or not a practicing homosexual should be in the pulpit or not. So even though they know their denominational leaders are corrupt and are not following the Holy Spirit, they still won't leave the denomination.

Even if God were to present Himself in a burning bush before this Hireling, and tell them to not be controlled by their denomination, they wouldn't listen.

Even if these Hirelings know one or all of their superiors are living an immoral ungodly lifestyle, these Hirelings don't dare challenge the person or persons in a Biblical and respectful way. Because they don't want to lose the comforts of a denomination. They don't have enough faith to believe that God would actually take care of them. So at times when they sense the denomination is controlling them more than God, they stay. Because after all, the denomination provides their salary, pension, housing, and they don't want to lose that. This is why they harm the congregation so much. Because they would rather be a people pleaser than a God pleaser. So they never challenge the congregation too much, and they don't want to upset the powers that be of the denomination. God's people need a real leader to take them to greener pastures, instead of a manager just doing the bare minimum.

Denominations Should Support The Call

A denomination can be a good thing if it actually supports the call of the pastor and the congregation. If the higher-ups are really spiritually mature, as in meeting the requirements of eldership as stated in Titus and 1 Timothy, then a pastor and local congregation can really benefit from a denomination's leadership. Moreover, some churches may be a part of certain denominations but they actually operate Biblically. They actually want to pursue the things of God. So if you are a part of a denomination where you are supported as a Biblical Kingdom-minded church, then, by all means, allow that denomination to help you. However, this is just not always the case. Denominations are often devoid of Kingdom-minded leaders. They may claim to have the "Spirit" or a great theological heritage, but they are now operating more on business principles and what's comfortable. So even when the Hirelings of a denomination sense this, they console themselves by saying, "Well...the Bible does say I should have counsel from many" (Proverbs 15:22). Yes, that's true...but what they should have is the right counsel. Nonetheless, because they cannot imagine what they would do without the denomination, due to their lack of faith, they just settle and let ungodly counsel pull their strings like a puppet.

Lacks Faith

I was talking to a pastor one day in his office. He told me that he had grown tired of the position he was in and felt like God had called him elsewhere. I told him that if he felt that way, he needed to pray about where God would be sending him next and to be obedient. He responded by saying, "I don't think I have enough education to leave the position I have now." I would like to say I was shocked by his response, but I wasn't. While I liked this pastor very much he was a slave to his denomination. And according to his denomination, upward mobility required him to get a PhD in theology and he only had a master's degree. So I told him, "If God is calling you somewhere else, it doesn't matter what your level of education is, you just need to move, apply, create, or do whatever it is God is telling you to do."

The Apostles did great things for Christ. They changed communities, and they didn't have a great education. People would see the marvelous acts and wisdom of the Apostles and be astonished! Look at what it says in Acts 4:13, *"When they saw the courage of Peter and John and realized that they were unschooled, ordinary men, they were astonished and they took note that these men had been with Jesus."* This is not to say that education is a bad thing. I am personally grateful for my theological training. But what is so significant about the Apostles like Peter and John, was not their education, but the fact that they had been with Jesus—having the power of the Holy Spirit and Jesus was enough! But this denominational pastor didn't realize that. He thought he needed more education. In other words, he didn't have faith. He was relying on his own abilities in scholarship to move him forward. It needs to be said that God may call people to get an education or even more education for ministry. However, it was clearly not the case with my pastoral friend that day. He just had more faith in his education and denomination than God.

I was talking to another denominational pastor who once said to me that, "He chose churches to serve earlier in his ministry that would be good moves for his children" In other words, if his children felt comfortable, if the salary was good for his kids to get everything they wanted, and if it was a good school system, then he opted for those churches. While this may seem noble, it is not right. As a parent myself, I want my children's needs to be taken care of, and I even want them to have extra from time to time— like vacations and things of that nature. However, Abraham didn't get this luxury with his family. They had to be wanderers who lived in tents. Imagine how hurt Abraham must have felt to almost sacrifice his son for God?

The point I'm making is that true pastors don't choose where to serve because of what's best for their children. On the contrary, true pastors know that the best place for their children to be is in the will of God. Even if that place doesn't seem favorable, true pastors will pack up their family and move to the area to which God has called them. Because the true pastor actually has faith that God will take care of them and their family.

So it is the "Denominational Servant Pastor" is someone who operates based on calculated risk, but not faith. Someone who takes a calculated risk is hoping to be lucky. However, faith is when someone trusts in the plans of God. And they may only have a hunch or a vision of what God wants them to do, but they step out in faith and do it anyway trusting in their God. They are not hoping to be lucky, they are believing that the same God that called them, will show them favor in the process. And personally, I would rather experience God's favor any day than to just be lucky. In essence, while the "Denominational Servant Pastor" would say they have faith, in reality, they have little to no faith. And why should they? They don't have to rely on God, instead they rely on the denomination. So while they preach and implore their congregations to have faith, they themselves lack it.

Status Quo

This Hireling is mediocre at best. They are comfortable and don't want things to change. If there is to be any change, they will accept it so long as it doesn't take them out of their comfort zone. While at times they want to be freer to follow the will of God, ultimately the comforts of a steady salary, pension, housing, and so on from a denomination that does the thinking for them, keeps them numb to God's will. Because of their mediocre relationship with Christ and practices, the congregation doesn't develop any high expectations in their own faith. This Hireling is mediocre, and the congregation begins to reflect their leader.

Some denominations, particularly of the traditional or mainline persuasion have something called the "lectionary." This is a resource with pre-selected verses for the Hireling to choose from to preach. While it was meant to be a helping tool, it becomes a crutch that the Hireling relies on more than God. The Lectionary is not inherently evil. And it can be used effectively. A pastor may use it for a season but hopefully is willing to preach outside of The Lectionary if God directs. But what happens to a lot of these Hirelings is that they only preach the pre-selected verses from The Lectionary for a particular Sunday. Moreover The Lectionary cycles through the exact same passages in a three-year cycle. And it doesn't cover the entirety of the Bible. Hence, when a Hireling relies totally on The Lectionary for preaching the Scriptures, the congregation doesn't have the opportunity to hear preaching from other passages. What if God wants the pastor to preach through the entire book of James, but the pastor doesn't because it's not in The Lectionary?

Again, The Lectionary can be used for a season should God will it. However, the pastor should be seeking God for what message and Scriptures to preach. Some preachers think you can preach any verse on any Sunday, and it's sufficient because it's the Word of God. However, they only say this because of ignorance, or they don't have a strong enough relationship with God to actually believe that He would tell them what to preach. Nevertheless, God will tell the preacher exactly what His people need to hear on Sunday, and the pastor needs to be obedient to preach it. Preachers like Peter, Stephen, John the Baptist, and the like, didn't have a lectionary. They spent time with God, and they preached what God put in their renewed hearts and minds.

This Hireling just wants to keep the programs of the church going because they want to report high numbers to their denomination. So they don't really want to practice accountability in their churches unless they really have to, because that might make people leave the church if they actually practice church discipline and accountability. Some of these Hirelings know that people in roles of leadership at their church are struggling with some serious sins. Serious enough that these individual leaders might need to step down from their roles of leadership and get spiritually healthy. Any real pastor would keep other leaders accountable because they love them and care more about their soul than their talents. However, the Hireling doesn't want to risk losing key leaders or people by confronting their sin. So they let the spiritually unhealthy leaders, or congregation members, continue on in their sin without lovingly confronting them. The Hireling thinks to themselves, "At least they are coming to church." Whereas if they really loved their congregation they would confront the sin that is hurting them. At the end of the day, this Hireling only wants to do what keeps them comfortable.

While I have written boldly about the damaging effects of a denomination, It's important for me to reiterate that a denomination can be helpful. Therefore, so long as a denomination actually supports the call of a pastor, supports God's agenda and not their own, and the congregation along with the pastor understand that a denomination assists the Kingdom of God but is not itself the Kingdom of God, then they can really help pastors and congregations. This is how a denomination could be helpful. However, I think more often than not, denominations just become distractions and interfere with the Kingdom of God. There were never supposed to be denominations. There is really only one Church that is following Christ. These churches may go by different names and are located all over the world, but they are Biblical, truly inspired by the Spirit, and establish the Kingdom wherever they may be.

Moreover, there is nothing wrong with a denomination or a church, providing a pastor with a salary, pension, insurance, etc. Real pastors put in a lot of work. However, these things shouldn't make the pastor comfortable to the point that the pastor no longer operates in faith, and loves comfort more than God. Beware of the Hirelings known as the "Denominational Servant Pastor," these Hirelings could make you just as faithless and mediocre as they are.

Solving The Problem

(This section will be at the end of every chapter to remind you of this truth.)

Dear reader, it's important for you to know that the "Denominational Servant Pastor" and the other pastors/ Hirelings mentioned in this book can absolutely be restored! God loves all people, including the pastors who might have lost their way. If you are a Christian leader and you feel convicted as you are reading the contents of this book, then you need to know that conviction doesn't mean condemnation (Romans 8:1). God loves you and is using this book as a wake-up call for you to turn some things around.

Therefore, while this book has/will diagnose the many problems behind the pulpit, let's not write these pastors off too quickly. God has provided a way for pastors to be restored. In chapter ten, I will reveal the solution for this pervasive problem in a section entitled, "Problem Solved." Because of Christ, there is hope.

FIVE

RIGID THEOLOGIAN PASTOR

This Hireling really understands a lot about theology. They believe in sound doctrine and they know their Bibles very well. There is so much to like about this type of Hireling. They know a little bit (or a lot) about the original languages of the Bible, such as Hebrew and Greek. They understand doctrinal truths such as Christology, Pneumatology, Eschatology, and so forth. They have studied apologetics, hermeneutics, homiletics, and ecclesiology. They are familiar with church polity and refer to their congregation as "the laity." They love to name drop and quote historical figures in the faith: They will talk about Thomas Aquinas, C. S. Lewis, John Calvin, John Wesley, Phoebe Palmer, St. Augustine, St. Anselm, and St. Teresa of Avila. In short, if you didn't understand any of these references and some of the language, trust me the "Rigid Theologian Pastor" does and will gladly teach you.

These people can be such a blessing to the body of Christ because we do need teachers who have a strong understanding of church history and sound doctrine. However, the problem with this Hireling is they only know how to relate to God from intellectual assent. This Hireling is like a Pharisee (Jewish religious and political teacher), having great knowledge but not having a great relationship with the Creator of such knowledge.

This type of Hireling can best be captured in Jesus' words to the Pharisees, *"'You are in error because you do not know the Scriptures or the power of God,'"* (Matthew 22:29). While the "Rigid Theologian Pastor" does have a lot of knowledge they don't really understand the nature of Scripture nor have they experienced the power of God. Let's examine this Hireling's error more clearly in the following:

Ignorant of the Nature of Scripture: Jesus once said to a group of Jewish leaders who were questioning His authority, *"You study the Scriptures diligently because you think that in them you have eternal life. These are the very Scriptures that testify about me, yet you refuse to come to me to have life,"* (John 5:39-40). In other words, the Scriptures should draw people closer to Christ, not just fill their heads with a bunch of knowledge—salvation is not found in how much Scripture you know, but in the Christ to whom the Scriptures point. The nature of Scripture is to draw us into a more faithful obedience towards Christ. But this Hireling doesn't understand that.

Ignorant of God's Power: I love the way the Apostle Paul addresses the Corinthian church. He says:

"And so it was with me, brothers and sisters. When I came to you, I did not come with eloquence or human wisdom as I proclaimed to you the testimony about God. For I resolved to know nothing while I was with you except Jesus Christ and him crucified. I came to you in weakness with great fear and trembling. My message and my preaching were not with wise and persuasive words, but with a demonstration of the Spirit's power so that your faith might not rest on human wisdom, but on God's power." (1 Corinthians 2:1-5)

These Hirelings assume that knowledge makes them more powerful, so they crave more of it. For they believe that the more facts, history, languages, and degrees they implement into their ministry is what makes them exceptional and approved by God. And the Bible docs say that we should be studious (2 Timothy 2:15). Nonetheless, it wasn't Peter and John's knowledge of Judaism that healed the beggar at the temple gate (Acts 3:6); it wasn't eloquent words that raised Lazarus from the dead (John 11:43); it was God's power. It's the power of God that breaks addictions, depression, and despair; it's the power of God that heals the blind, sick, and broken; it's the power of God that transforms our sinful nature into the righteousness of Christ (2 Corinthians 5:21). The Apostle Paul was also an educated man. His education did aid him in his discourses about Christ, but he ultimately understood, it was a relationship with Christ and the power of God that changed peoples lives, not just head knowledge.

Self-Sufficient

The Hireling that is the "Rigid Theologian Pastor" could be great for their congregation if they had more to offer than just mental assent. Every congregation has real issues, and they need a pastor that prays while actually believing the power of God can and will change their lives. It's not that this Hireling doesn't pray for their congregation—they really do—but they are just going through the motions. Prayer is almost like a mental exercise for these Hirelings instead of flowing out of a vibrant relationship with Christ.

It's almost like saying the "Pledge of Allegiance." Ideally, we all know it and can recite it, but do we always recite it with a passion and a true connection to what we are saying? Perhaps some do, but not all. For some, the "Pledge of Allegiance" is a mental jog that we quoted in school but haven't given much thought about since then. Likewise, these Hirelings pray to God, but they don't give much thought to what they say; they don't wait in deep anticipation, believing that God is really going to act on their prayers. They would much rather get back to studying Scripture, church history, languages, etc. because they feel in control of their own studies. They can harness and interpret the Scripture for any given situation; they can use what other important church figures have said in the past or present; they can use church tradition to support their conclusion. This Hireling simply goes through the motions of prayer instead of actually believing that God will intervene; they struggle with depending on God in prayer because their intellectual exploits have made them feel self-sufficient. While they would never admit it, they rely on their own brain power. They could accomplish a lot more for their congregation if they spent just as much time praying as they did studying…but they don't believe that.

They hurt the congregation because there is no Holy Spirit power behind their ministry. When Peter preached his sermon on the day of Pentecost there was so much power behind it that people were convicted and three thousand people gave their lives to Christ that day (Acts 2:14-41). But not so with these Hirelings. They fail their congregation because they are not relying on the Holy Spirit's power to help the congregation. Their leadership skills, preaching, and pastoral counseling is all driven from the intellect and is not inspired. If a person expressed what the experience of this Hireling's ministry is like, they would say, "The preacher gives a lot of great information, the sermon is eloquently worded, but I'm not inspired at all. I don't sense the Holy Spirit in what this preacher does." People need to experience the power of God in our churches, not just the intellect.

No New Or Greater Advancements

Aside from a future dwelling place with God (Heaven), this Hireling assumes the best has already happened. In a real sense, they are stuck in the past. They believe the best revelation revealed for the Church, theology, and the Christian lifestyle has already been taught and practiced. But there's still so much to pursue. Now before you assume the worst about what I just said, let me clarify some things. I absolutely agree that the 66 books of the Bible are all that is needed for the Christian. The Word of God as we have it today is God's will for humanity revealed. What the Bible has to say about lifestyles, religion, morality, eternity, etc., is sufficient, inspired, authoritative, and powerful— it is God's Word to us and for us—it need not be changed. The Bible even gives a strong warning for those who manipulate and change the Scripture for their own purposes (Revelation 22:19).

What I am saying is that we shouldn't look at church history or what happened in the Scripture and assume, "That is not for us today." What those earlier Old and New Testament followers did in the name of God, should still be happening today and with an even greater impact. That is what I mean by saying, "There's still so much more to pursue." If it's in the Scripture, we can do it and even more so. Think about all those awesome miracles and acts of justice Jesus accomplished in His lifetime on earth. He impacted entire communities and the world. And yet, Jesus told His disciples and us today that we would do even greater works than Him (John 14:12).

According to Jesus, we can see greater miracles; we can influence governments; we can grow more in knowledge and relationship with the Holy Spirit. But this Hireling doesn't believe this. They just believe that what has been done, is done. They give the congregation some interesting intellectual information that is helpful to a degree, but the congregation struggles to believe for any supernatural, new, practical, and exciting advancements for the Kingdom of God. They are lulled into a Christian lifestyle where they are spiritually fat and happy with all the knowledge they have been taught by their Hireling, but they don't really advance the Kingdom of God.

They Don't Believe In The Supernatural/Miracles

Every Christian believes in the miraculous. If you are a Christian who says you don't believe in miracles, you are either deceived or you are lying. I do not care what Christian denomination or association you belong to—when a Christian claims not to believe in miracles or the supernatural that is an oxymoron. I can prove that all

Christians believe in the supernatural. Let's just name a few basic and orthodox beliefs that all Christians believe. (if you do not believe these, then you may want to evaluate whether or not you are indeed a Christian):

Virgin Birth: A woman conceived a child without ever being sexually intimate with a man

Jesus: He claimed to be the Son of God and even was God, He was a Jewish carpenter, a faith healer, the Savior of the world, and He died a criminals death on a cross

Resurrection: Jesus rose from the dead

Prayer: People sit in a space and talk to a God they cannot see

When you look at this list of beliefs that are basic to the Christian faith, does any of it make sense? The answer is no! When you actually stop and think about the basic Christian beliefs it sounds strange. Just think it over…if you are a Christian then you believe that a Jewish carpenter, all the way from the Middle East, saved your life by dying on a cross. He then rose from the dead and went to be with God the Father. This actually sounds like a joke. A woman conceiving a child without being sexually intimate with a man…that is not logically possible (especially in that day, there was no in vitro back then).

And now you, as a Christian, sit in a church on Sunday to celebrate a Jewish man who died on the cross for your sins. There are even these weird times when the pastor dunks you in water and you eat a small piece of bread with juice some Sundays. You also pray to this God that you cannot see! This all sounds like fantasy; it sounds goofy; it sounds impossible because it should be. It is supernatural. And for those of us who have been saved by the Gospel, we understand what it all means and we know it's true—Hallelujah. Even the Apostle Paul once claimed that what we believe seems like foolishness to the world (1 Corinthians 1:18).

Dear Christian, somehow you have been duped into believing that your Christian faith is normal and it's not. Do you see now why every Christian believes in the supernatural and the miraculous? If you have been saved and are practicing basic Christian beliefs you are radical, charismatic, and some people think you are strange. Since we now have established that you believe in the supernatural, why do you struggle to believe in speaking in tongues, healings, and spiritual gifts? Are these more radical than you sitting in a room speaking to a God you cannot see and believing a man resurrected from the dead? The answer is, no. These are just as radical as the basic Christian beliefs. There is no "normal" branch of Christianity, we are all weird. God does work in supernatural ways today. Don't let the bad examples of people who have abused and manipulated the supernatural workings of God, or this Hireling who wants to make you believe that everything is mental assent, keep you from increasing your faith to believe God for the supernatural.

Those early Apostles experienced a lot of the supernatural because they actually believed. Think of how much easier it was for them to believe in the supernatural. The majority of the Apostles actually walked with Jesus. They saw Jesus do incredible things, so by the time Jesus left to be with the Father, they had a recent reference of Jesus operating in the supernatural, and they were willing to believe and practice it. However, now, about 2,000 years since Jesus left the earth, and some people are not sure if God still does the supernatural. Not many churches seek to practice or equip people to function in spiritual gifts. So because Christians haven't been exposed to it enough and they don't have many present references for it, they don't pursue it. But I'm telling you, God still does miracles today and equips His people to do the same… I've seen the sick recover; I've seen people speak in new tongues; I've seen people prophesy with accuracy; I've seen demons cast out from people.

We need the power of the Holy Spirit in the church today. But this Hireling only teaches the congregation that everything is mental assent. Some people sit in this Hireling's church, starving to talk about the supernatural, starving to be engaged more, but this Hireling only tickles their intellect. The "Rigid Theologian Pastor" does not like ambiguity. They want everything to fit into a scholarly approach to the Bible. So when they come across a supernatural event in the Scripture, they preach and teach such event as just a symbol or meaning for something within humanity's scope. But my question to this Hireling would be…what if God actually wants His people to not only be intelligent but to operate with the power and demonstration of the Spirit?

Molehills Into Mountains

One of the biggest problems of this Hireling is that they turn what is minor into a major. We have all heard the saying, "You're making mountains out of molehills." And this is what happens. Because they love to scrutinize Scripture, history, and tradition, sometimes they turn subjects that don't affect a person's salvation or sanctification, into issues that do. For example, this Hireling may claim that there is only one translation of the Bible to read from. The Hireling may also be a preacher who believes pastors should be in a robe or a suit. The Hireling may even love more of what a particular famous theologian/pastor said about the Scripture than the Scripture itself. In other words, this Hireling only believes certain Scriptures are more validated because a famous theologian/pastor like John Wesley or Smith Wigglesworth talked about such Scriptures.

None of the examples I listed are essential to your salvation and walk with Christ. But this Hireling will make you think so. They say things like, "You should only be reading from this translation of the Bible" or "According to church tradition and John Wesley, this is why we believe this" or "Preachers that don't preach in a robe are disrespectful to God because that's how the saints of the past honored God." While it may sound like what they are saying is Scriptural, it is just their opinion.

My personal opinion is that there are many good Bible translations and if a person really wants the best version of the Bible, they should learn and read it in the original languages of Hebrew, Greek, and some Aramaic. Moreover, I like preaching in regular clothes because a robe makes me feel like a judge and a suit makes me feel like a businessman of which I am neither. So long as my clothing doesn't distract people from receiving the Gospel message, I'm happy to preach in my plaid shirts and blue jeans. However, if some preachers like their suits or their robes, they are welcome to them. I also like many historical and influential church figures. I read up on them regularly. If I do mention a famous theologian it's to help better explain a Biblical point, but I don't name drop them to validate the Scripture, the Holy Spirit is the one that validates the Scripture.

Why am I going through all this trouble with these examples? Because I'm trying to show you how trivial this is. If it's not a salvation or sanctification issue, who cares? The translation of the Bible, your favorite theologian, the style of church you like, etc., cannot save you. Only Christ is the Savior. But at their worst, this Hireling will have you basing your entire salvation on what denomination, historical theologian, style, or the version of the Bible you subscribe to—this Hireling often runs the risk of becoming legalistic and self-righteous. Whereby you must do everything based on the way they see it. And some of what they see is Biblical but sometimes it just their opinion.

Again, it needs to be said that we need sound doctrine in the Church, we need to look at Church history, but the Church also needs the supernatural. The Church needs more than just mental exercises. People are dealing with some serious stuff and need the power of God. What this Hireling doesn't realize is that the Church of Jesus Christ is called to be both scholarly and supernatural. Do not let your faith become cold, calculated, and calloused to the Holy Spirit because of this Hireling.

Solving The Problem

(This section will be at the end of every chapter to remind you of this truth.)

Dear reader, it's important for you to know that the "Rigid Theologian Pastor" and the other pastors/Hirelings mentioned in this book can absolutely be restored! God loves all people, including the pastors who might have lost their way. If you are a Christian leader and you feel convicted as you are reading the contents of this book, then you need to know that conviction doesn't mean condemnation (Romans 8:1). God loves you and is using this book as a wake-up call for you to turn some things around.

Therefore, while this book has/will diagnose the many problems behind the pulpit, let's not write these pastors off too quickly. God has provided a way for pastors to be restored. In chapter ten, I will reveal the solution for this pervasive problem in a section entitled, "Problem Solved." Because of Christ, there is hope.

SIX

WOUNDED PASTOR

I will step lightly as we talk about this Hireling because this type is already hurt, and I don't want to add insult to injury. However, these debunked pastors let their hurt feelings dictate their ministry more than God. What is so disappointing is that they were at one point passionate about ministry. They were close to God. They were anointed and talented for the ministry to which God called them. But somewhere along the process, they got hindered by their hurt feelings.

While people may not realize this, pastors—not all the time, but sometimes—take blows and shots from the people they are trying to minister to and even demonic forces. Some years ago, I was serving as the pastor of a traditional church, even though I didn't quite fit the bill of being a traditional pastor. Sometimes I would wear a traditional suit and other times I would not. And while every Sunday is important in that we gather to celebrate Christ, some Sunday services are especially highlighted for specific events related to Biblical festivals or the life of Christ (E.g., Pentecost, Christmas, Easter, etc.).

One special day in the Christian/Church calendar is Palm Sunday. This is the Sunday before Easter, and it commemorates when Jesus entered Jerusalem and the masses laid palm branches at His feet (Matthew 21:1-11). It's an exciting day in the Church, as it recognizes that Jesus is getting ready to go to the cross for our sins. So on one Palm Sunday, I decided to preach in a pair of nice blue jeans instead of a suit. After service, there was a lady in the kitchen telling other members how annoyed she was because I wore jeans on Palm Sunday. My wife overheard her gossiping to other members: "I cannot believe pastor Brian wore Jeans! It's Palm Sunday."

At the time, discovering that this member was talking poorly about me was slightly hurtful. I did the funeral for her father, I counseled her through some tough moments, prayed for her many times. And yet, none of that mattered to her. She was simply offended because I wore jeans on Palm Sunday. But regardless of her gossip about me, I still was gracious towards her. Because at a certain point, a pastor realizes that even though people reject you, what you do is actually for God. While it is true that Jesus went to the cross because He loved us, the main reason is that Christ wanted to please His heavenly Father (John 5:19).

Jesus took the criticism from religious leaders and various people. He was beaten, mocked, rejected, and murdered. And there were times when Jesus' feelings tried to deter

Him from the mission the Father gave Him. We see in the Garden of Gethsemane Jesus resisting feelings of discouragement and perhaps fear. In prayer to God the Father, He actually asks for the burden of suffering for the sins of the world to be removed from Him. But He resolved to do the will of the Father (Luke 22:42). In other words, If Jesus would have acted on the feelings He felt in the Garden of Gethsemane, He would have never gone to the cross.

Jesus would have had every right to give up on humanity. We didn't deserve a Savior such as He. The world had mistreated and abused Him. Why die for a world that had rejected Him? Once more, it is because He wanted to please the Father, and He didn't let hurt feelings control Him. The true pastor understands this: That even though as a pastor there will be times in which people reject you, gossip about you, criticize you, and will not appreciate you, you continue to serve and love God's people because as a pastor it is your worship towards God! If Jesus could overcome backstabbers like Judas, doubters like Thomas, enraged people like Peter, then ideally, pastors should be able to overcome the people, who come and go throughout their ministry that have unkind remarks, gestures, intentions, and actions. I am not saying pastors should be a doormat and not create healthy boundaries of respect and order. Nonetheless, pastors shouldn't be surprised when someone from the congregation or in the community betrays them. If it happened to Jesus, then it will happen to you dear pastor. Unfortunately, this Hireling forgets that everything they do in ministry should be for God. So they get caught up in their hurt feelings and become ineffective for the calling. And we all know that sometimes, our feelings can deceive us.

Wounded By Spiritual Forces

This Hireling has forgotten that the real battle is not with people because *"...our struggle is not against flesh and blood, but against the rulers, against the authorities, against the powers of this dark world and against the spiritual forces of evil in the heavenly realms,"* (Ephesians 6:12). This Hireling forgets that their congregation members may be dealing with and/or influenced by demons. So instead of praying for the congregation to be set free from demonic influences, they take the comments of the negative congregation member or their lack of appreciation personally. However, Jesus—not being controlled by His feelings—didn't allow what people did to affect His ministry, but rather He attacked the demonic spirits that were influencing people.

For example, one time the disciple Peter tried to talk Jesus out of dying for the sins of the world. But Jesus looks at Peter and says *"Get behind me, Satan"* (Matthew 16:21-23). Peter was influenced by the Devil at that moment to try to deter and distract Jesus from fulfilling the mission God the Father gave Him. Hence, Jesus—being aware of Satan's plot and influence on Peter's life—speaks directly against the Devil working in Peter. In other words, Jesus wasn't upset with Peter, He loved Peter so He didn't take it personally, rather He was annoyed and took authority over the Devil who had influenced him.

The reality is you can be close to God just like Peter was, and still be used by the Devil. You may be a Christian who loves God, but every so often the Devil influences you to do things that are not of God. And at times, unbeknownst to the typical congregation member, the Devil might influence him/her to say or do something negative to the pastor. The Devil knew he couldn't influence Jesus, so the Devil tried to influence Jesus through somebody Jesus loved, namely Peter. I have said a lot about pastors and their shattered pulpits. However, there also might be shattered pews in which Christians are being used by the Devil to make life hard on the pastor.

Nonetheless, these Hirelings hurt the congregation, because they begin to see the members as the enemy instead of seeing the true enemy: the Devil. As a parent of four children, I know that in my interactions with my young children I am the mature one. And as such, I will overcome whatever insults or defiant behavior they display because I am the parent in charge. Hence, there are times where I limit or restrict my kids from doing certain things because it is for their safety or discipline. But because my children don't always understand that what I'm doing is for their good, they may respond in a fit of anger and say, "I don't like you, dad!" This always makes me laugh because they just don't know how much I love and care about them. They just don't see the bigger picture like I do as the parent. So I don't take it personally! I continue to love, care, and develop my children.

Likewise, pastors should be one of the most, if not the most spiritually mature person in their church. They shouldn't take it personally when the congregation does or says things inappropriately. They should stand firm, be consistent, be loving, be caring, be righteous, and be a leader in spite of opposition. There will always be a Judas (somebody influenced by the Devil) or more than one in every congregation...even Jesus had a Judas in His camp. But you don't let it stop you from loving the people. The enemy is not people; it is the Devil. Jesus was so aware of this that even when He was on the cross, He didn't use that time to condemn people. No, the Bible says that He forgave the people. *"'Jesus said, 'Father, forgive them, for they do not know what they are doing,'"* (Luke 23:34a).

Preaches/Teaches From Disappointment

This Hireling has been so consumed by their personal disappointment and pain that their preaching and teaching often reflect this hurt. While they may not realize it, this Hireling is always coming across to the congregation as a victim. So instead of the congregation being inspired by the pastor's preaching, they feel sorry for their pastor. This Hireling consistently brings up in their sermon and teaching all the wrong that was done in their life or they allude to it. Now if some of you have a healthy pastor this may all sound foreign to you. But honestly, wounded pastors are constantly referencing something negative that has happened or is happening to them.

For example, I have known of churches that have had some terrible splits that have wounded a pastor. What I mean is that a divisive person enters a church, and never intends to be a faithful supportive member. If they really don't like the style, function, or pastor of a church they should belong to another church to which perhaps God is calling them. However, they stay and complain about the pastor, the music, the building, the programs, and so on. The divisive person ultimately gets some of the immature congregation to agree with their complaints, and they all leave the church. But these people don't leave quietly, they leave in a loud destructive way. The find an excuse to leave by typically blaming the pastor and other leaders for things they did not do—they lie.

Hence, if the pastor is not strong enough, they will not overcome this wound— they won't heal. They are hurting because the divisive person caused people to gossip, slander, and lie about the pastor. The people the pastor cared for, betray the pastor (sounds a lot like what Jesus experienced). Unfortunately, because this pastor hasn't healed, they might go the next several years referencing what those deviant people did in the church. It seems like at least once a month in their preaching or in meetings they will find a way to bring up the hurtful past. Meanwhile, the congregation that remains, wants their pastor back! They don't want to keep hearing how those nasty people caused division in the church, they want to go forward. The people that stayed after the church split are there because they still believe in their pastor. But now, pastors who have had this experience struggle to believe in themselves because so many people gossiped and deserted them.

A church split is just one of the many examples that cause a pastor to become wounded. Now it needs to be said that every pastor that is passionate about their ministry, will at one point be wounded for some reason. Trying to work with other people and dealing with demonic forces, you are certain to get a few wounds. But a true Pastor will not stay wounded. Just like Jesus Christ resurrected from the grave, the true pastor heals and bounces back.

Started With Hurt Feelings

Not every wounded pastor was called and became wounded in the process of pastoring. On the contrary, there are some of these Hirelings that became a pastor because of their wounds. They assume that because they have experienced pain in life they should get behind a pulpit somewhere and help people. This type of thinking frustrates me because you don't become a pastor because of life experience or because you are a nice person that wants to help people. It's not your wounds (or life experience) that makes you qualified for ministry. And if you haven't healed from your wounds you will just hurt the congregation.

The truth be told, sometimes these Hirelings get behind a pulpit because they are looking for a place to feel good about themselves and to share their pity party with others. In other words, they are actually still wounded from whatever life circumstance that has taken place in their lives. It could be that they were abused as children, neglected by their parents, bullied, etc. So they subconsciously assume that the way to escape their painful past or present is to get behind a pulpit and minister to people. They haven't healed from their wounds but they think that by helping others heal from their own wounds, they will find healing in the process. They are out to prove that they are nice people that have something to offer because their wounds tell them otherwise. Hence, this Hireling becomes codependent on the congregation instead of God. They love when they help a church member who says "thank you…you're an amazing pastor" or "I feel good when I am around you." This is not to say that we shouldn't be complimenting and encouraging the pastor. And at times even true pastors will have moments of vulnerability and share some of the areas where they have been wounded. However, this is what this Hireling secretly obsesses about. They just want the praise and pity of people. They are like the kid that was always picked last to play a game, and the kid gets older and wants to prove why he or she should never have been overlooked. It's a shame that God's love isn't enough for this Hireling.

Evidence Of The Wounded Pastor

Bitter: This Hireling demonstrates their bitterness in a couple of ways. 1) At times their bitterness shows if the congregation isn't giving them a significant amount of praise. 2) If this Hireling has been so hurt by what the congregation has or hasn't done, they will be bitter regardless of how appreciative the congregation is. Basically, while trying to care for the congregation they simultaneously see them as their enemy. So encounters with this Hireling is bittersweet. In essence, it seems likes your pastor cares for you, but you also feel like your pastor is offended by your presence.

Isolation: It's like they don't fully trust people. They have been so hurt that they want to control more than anything else because that way they will ensure they won't be injured again. They may produce great messages and have a few good leadership skills, but they don't know how to empower people. In short, they have become cowardly. Underneath the surface, they think, "If I empower people too much they might abuse that power and hurt me again." This Hireling becomes isolated in their thoughts, feelings, and their plans. You never feel like this Hireling believes in what you can do because they subconsciously want you to be below them. Because after all, the people that hurt this Hireling before, thought they were above or better than them.

Exhausted: Any true pastor will get tired from time to time and need rest. However, this Hireling is tired because they are running off of pride and not the inspiration of the Holy Spirit. They have convinced themselves to be tougher and stronger...that to keep themselves from being hurt they need to appear confident and capable. Their wound hasn't healed, but they soothe themselves by thinking, "People don't deserve me!" or "I'm more called than anybody else." They have become so victimized in their mind that their introspective needs to be recalibrated. In other words, even at times when they need to make changes they don't because they assume it's everyone else's fault. Even though deep down on the inside they know things are falling apart, they don't know where to turn to alleviate the burdens. This Hireling is exhausted and should take a break from ministry or step down to a ministry role that has less responsibility until they get healed.

Due to the wounded nature of this Hireling, the congregation becomes stagnant and bored because the pastor is uninspired and ineffective. The congregation is really loyal to this Hireling because they know their pastor has been hurt. Apart from their wounded nature, the congregation knows their pastor is a good person—there are flashes where their pastor shows great promise. And some people of this congregation begin to feel the nudge from God to be at another church with a pastor that will inspire and challenge them. But, the congregation feels guilty about leaving and feels stuck. Because if they leave this Hireling, they feel like they add to the hurt their pastor has already experienced. But if they stay, they continue to drown in the victimhood status of the Hireling. Unfortunately, the congregation begins to adopt the bitter, isolated, and exhausted nature of the Hireling, and begin to blame some boogieman out in the world for why the church isn't filled with the vibrancy of the Spirit anymore. When the truth is that this Hireling should resign or repent and begin to heal for the sake of themselves and the church they are leading.

Dear Church, Don't Make It Tougher For The Pastor!

In the book of Hebrews, there is an admonishment or instruction for the Church: *"Have confidence in your leaders and submit to their authority, because they keep watch over you as those who must give an account. Do this so that their work will be a joy, not a burden, for that would be of no benefit to you,"* (Hebrews 13:17).

This passage teaches not to create unnecessary burdens for Christian leaders. Therefore, dear Christian, you need to know that if you have a true pastor, they are working hard for you. They are praying for you regularly; they feel pain when they hear about your misfortune; they have embraced you like family. The true pastor is also trying to equip you to have an impact in the world. If your minister is a real called pastor, then your minister is working for God. And attempting to support your Christian life.

So please, don't make the calling and mission of the pastor any harder than it needs to be. If you do not intend to follow your pastor's leadership, then you should not be at that church. Don't allow the Devil to influence you.

Because when you gossip and slander a pastor who is really called from God, just know that one day we will all have to give an account for our actions.

I say this because sometimes an anointed and called pastor gets wounded because the congregation fights every advancement this pastor tries to make for the church and the Kingdom of God. Hence, some people will never be a good church member because they don't want to follow the leadership of any pastor. Basically, unbeknownst to the obstinate church member, they are sent by the Devil to cause distraction in local churches. However, if you attend a church where you feel like the called and anointed pastor isn't for you…then okay…you need to belong to a church where there is a called pastor that would challenge and love you. There is a church where God is calling you to be in community and serve. Basically, just because a pastor isn't for you, doesn't mean said pastor isn't called by God, so avoid gossip.

Peter Or Judas?

If I could speak to this Hireling directly I would say, "Who do you want to be? Peter or Judas?" Peter and Judas both experienced a wound. They both were hurt by betraying the Savior. Peter denied Him three times and Judas sold Him out for thirty pieces of silver. Peter felt wounded for betraying the Lord but ultimately received forgiveness, repented, and became a powerhouse for the Kingdom of God. Sadly, this was not the case for Judas. He was so wounded for having betrayed the Savior that he decided to commit suicide.

What I am trying to say is that the wounded pastor can become healed, they can be restored to a place of great ministry. If they are willing to take some time off, be healed, confess, repent, and be forgiven, God can restore them to great health just like the Apostle Peter. But because of stubbornness, a lot of these Hirelings have bought into the lie that they can never be healed. So their ministry has the stench of death around it just like Judas.

These Hirelings oftentimes do not have strong mentors in their life and if they do, they're not really deeply connected to their said mentor—it's just a formality that makes it seem like they have accountability. But a pastor always needs a pastor. Somebody that can share the burden with them. If this Hireling doesn't get whole, they will end up hurting the congregation and they usually have a lot of hidden sins like pornography, stealing, or improperly using the church's money, etc. This Hireling's ministry doesn't have to end tragically like Judas. They can be like Peter and make amends where they can, take some time off, get healed, and if God calls them back to the pulpit, they will come back with the power of the Holy Spirit and be a powerhouse like Peter. But if this Hireling is too stubborn to be changed by the power of God...watch yourself... these types of Hirelings will make you as wounded as they are.

Solving The Problem

(This section will be at the end of every chapter to remind you of this truth.)

Dear reader, it's important for you to know that the "Wounded Pastor" and the other pastors/Hirelings mentioned in this book can absolutely be restored! God loves all people, including the pastors who might have lost their way. If you are a Christian leader and you feel convicted as you are reading the contents of this book, then you need to know that conviction doesn't mean condemnation (Romans 8:1). God loves you and is using this book as a wake-up call for you to turn some things around.

Therefore, while this book has/will diagnose the many problems behind the pulpit, let's not write these pastors off too quickly. God has provided a way for pastors to be restored. In chapter ten, I will reveal the solution for this pervasive problem in a section entitled, "Problem Solved." Because of Christ, there is hope.

SEVEN

NON-CHRISTIAN PASTOR

The thought of there being a pastor behind a pulpit that is not Christian sounds absurd, but it's unfortunately true. How can this happen? Because people think that if a person is motivated, kind, skilled, and/or has a great following, then they must be a person from God. But let's not forget that Satan is also motivated, skilled, pretends to be kind, and has a great following. This is how the Devil gets us to fall into temptation. He shows up to the Garden of Eden, appearing to have the best of intentions, he seems kind, is obviously skillful, and deceives Adam and Eve into believing that eating of the fruit is a good thing. Hence, the Hireling known as the "Non-Christian Pastor" has God's people eating or consuming a lot of junk that is not godly or Biblical.

These Hirelings weasel themselves into a church and cause the congregation to worship false gods. Because they don't know the real God, they have the congregation chasing every falsehood under the sun. While all these Hirelings I have mentioned in this book thus far are problematic, I honestly do not know which is worst when it comes to the Hireling known as the "Wolf In Sheep's Clothing" or this one. Because the "Non-Christian Pastor" and the "Wolf In

Sheep's Clothing" cause severe confusion and damage to the body of Christ. They both are extremely manipulative when it comes to the Scripture, and are deeply entangled with demons.

Let me make something exclusively clear. There are certain foundational truths that one must adhere to in order to be Christian (E.g., virgin birth, sanctification, etc.). But the one that is the biggest, the most glaring, and is required in order to have a relationship with God that leads to eternal life is...hmmm...let me use a fancy word for emphasis: CHRISTOLOGY! This is Christian doctrine that has to do with the person and work of Jesus Christ. Basically, this is about who Jesus is and what He did or does!

Christology is more than just your belief that Jesus exists, but rather, what do you believe about His nature and purpose, and does it match the Christian Scripture? The "Non-Christian Pastor" is deceived by demons (as we all once were before Christ entered our lives) because they think that just their belief in God or Jesus is enough. Not so! Because the Bible says, *"You believe that there is one God. Good! Even the demons believe that—and shudder,"* (James 2:19). Demons believe that God or Jesus exists, but they don't willingly submit to His Lordship. Likewise, these Hirelings believe in Jesus, but they don't truly understand the person and nature of Christ, and therefore, don't really submit to Christ.

These Hirelings damage their congregation severely because they don't know the God they are talking about. The false god they present is not the one presented in the Scripture, but what they perceive for their own liking. The congregation adopts the belief system of this Hireling, and thus develops this shallow, whimsical, intellectual, spiritual, but not Christian type of belief. This is a very dangerous Hireling because their teachings kill a person's spirit. It's one thing to kill the body because it's going to die anyway. But to destroy someone's spirit is villainy at the highest level for that has eternal implications. What Satan did in the Garden was to make humanity spiritually dead to God! And that's exactly what this Hireling does.

Believes In Multiple Ways To Be Saved

The Bible is very clear that Jesus is exclusively the Savior of the world! He is not a way, but He is the way to God! In fact, He is God. Listen to how Scripture talks about the brilliance of Christ:

"The Son is the image of the invisible God, the firstborn over all creation. For in him all things were created: things in heaven and on earth, visible and invisible, whether thrones or powers or rulers or authorities; all

things have been created through him and for him. He is before all things, and in him all things hold together. And he is the head of the body, the church; he is the beginning and the firstborn from among the dead, so that in everything he might have the supremacy. For God was pleased to have all his fullness dwell in him, and through him to reconcile to himself all things, whether things on earth or things in heaven, by making peace through his blood, shed on the cross" (Colossians 1:15-20).

If you are truly a believer in Christ, there's something about this passage you just read that makes you joyful. There is something that makes you say on the inside, "Yes and amen! What I have just read is true." When you have been truly saved, Jesus means a whole lot...or better yet... He means everything to you. As a Christian, you know that He was and is God in the flesh (John 1:1-14). You know that He is the Savior of the world and there is no one else like Him (Acts 4:11-12). However, this Hireling doesn't believe in the exclusivity of Jesus Christ. This Hireling believes in Him but ultimately believes there are multiple gods or ways to eternity.

For this Hireling, God can be represented in many religions. They believe Jesus is one of the many names for God. They assume that when you talk about Buddha, Allah, etc., you are talking about the same eternal being known as God. Hence, according to this Hireling, all forms of faith or religious expression lead to eternity or God. So while these Hirelings view themselves as Christian pastors, they could have just as easily been a leader of Hinduism, Jainism, Sikhism, or some type of New Age belief system.

While they are in the position of a Christian pastor, they actually view themselves as "spiritual." Meaning that any belief or religion that connects one with a version of god is right and good (any other god that is not the God we find in the Scripture is just a demon in disguise). And in their attempt to blend all these faiths into one, this Hireling actually insults the participants of these different belief systems who actually understand the nuances and practices of their religion/belief systems.

So let me be intentionally dogmatic here. Regardless of what one may say or conclude, the Christian Bible makes no room or exceptions for who Jesus is. Biblically speaking, there is one God who exists eternally in the Triune nature of God the Father, God the Son, and God the Holy Spirit. And Jesus is Lord of all. There are not multiple gods or entry points to eternity, there is but one— Jesus Christ. Beyond understanding who Christ is, there are certain expectations, norms, and privileges the Christian experiences because of grace and faith experienced in Jesus Christ. What I'm trying to say is this: If a person wants to get behind a pulpit and preach about anything other than the supremacy and exclusivity of

Christ, and deviates from the Biblical teachings of Christian doctrine, behavior, and affections, then that preacher is a "Non-Christian Pastor." They are preaching a faith or belief system that is not Christian, and therefore not of the God we find in the Bible. If this Hireling wants to hold onto their false beliefs, they are welcome to do so, but let's not call it Christian or salvific in any form.

God the Father, did something very hard for any father to do. He allowed His Son to be punished for the world. Jesus was innocent; He did no wrong, and yet, according to the Christian Scripture, God the Father poured out His wrath on His own Son, for our sake. God the Father gave up His own Son for me and you. I should have been punished for my sins, but Jesus was willing to be punished and die in my place. And now because of the sacrifice Jesus made on the cross, I am now filled with the Holy Spirit! Hallelujah! And destined to spend eternity with God. Who am I, to spit on what God did for me by acting like Christ's sacrifice is just one of the many ways to salvation? No, it was Christ who saved me, it was Christ that changed me, I will not stop talking about the goodness of Christ. I didn't save myself, it was the grace of God. But this Hireling insults the sacrifice of Christ by nonchalantly claiming, "There are multiple ways to God."

Questions The Authority Of The Scriptures

At this point, it shouldn't be surprising that this Hireling doesn't view the Bible as supremely authoritative. Due to their belief of multiple pathways to God, they believe the Bible is only one written expression of the will of God. This is implored in beliefs systems such as Mormonism in that they believe there are multiple testaments of the Bible beyond the Old and New Testament (they also have beliefs that are not congruent with Christian Scripture). Even Universalist (belief that all people will be saved whether they want to or not) types of churches do not necessarily esteem the Bible as the only authoritative written form of God's Word.

Moreover, the Catholic church has a section included in their Bible called the Apocrypha. The Apocrypha is in addition to the 66 books comprised to make up the Bible. These are writings the Catholic church and perhaps others believe should be considered as Scripture. However, the Protestant Bible (meaning non-Catholic Bible) doesn't esteem the Apocrypha as divine Scripture, because there is some discrepancy concerning origins and authenticity of these books. Some Christians believe the Apocrypha does not contradict the basic understanding of the Christian Bible. Nonetheless, I am convinced that the 66 books we have of the Christian Bible are all we need to understand the will of God.

In short, the true believer is confident that the Christian Scripture from Genesis to Revelation is the authentic Word of God. A Christian can read sound Biblical commentaries, they can listen to historic or present Christian authors, speakers, and preachers concerning the Bible. These can be tools that we, as Christians, use to get us to think about the Bible, to start discussions, and to deepen our thoughts and faith. But if a so-called pastor, such as the "Non-Christian pastor," gets behind the pulpit while preaching and teaching doctrine or principles that are not reflected in the Scripture…that person is a heretic.

This Hireling literally believes that because one can find some Christian truth in other spiritual books that it must be just as authoritative as the Bible. They claim that all truth belongs to God, so they believe that any spiritual book that promotes goodwill and life with God is truth. And I would absolutely agree that all truth belongs to God. But a partial truth is not the truth. Other religions or belief systems may have partial truth. But ultimately, the continued and beautiful narrative of a worthy God reaching out and loving an unworthy people (humanity) cannot be illustrated in an anymore compelling, authentic, and supernaturally transforming way than it is in the Christian Scripture. Unlike other religions where it is humanity trying to reach or gain God's approval or achieve some type of euphoric spiritual state of being; our God came to us, and died for us. Christianity unlike other religions or belief systems is not about how good we are; it's about how good God has been to us! And because of having received God's love and goodness we then do good works because we are motivated by God's love for us and moving through us to others. The Christian is not trying to earn God's love by being good or better than other people, but a Christian does good after being saved and knowing that God is with them.

Hence, you can find morality, principles, and interesting things in other spiritual books. As a matter of fact, I have looked into other religious books and found them to be interesting. Nonetheless, it does not provide the truth that sets people free. Only Christ is mighty to save.

One time I had a serious conversation with one of these Non-Christian pastors in seminary. We were both in seminary studying to be effective pastors in the future. We were taking the same courses, and I knew we had completely different views on Scripture. I thought it would be interesting for me to sit down with someone who had different views on Scripture than I did. So we met over lunch one time and we discussed an array of Biblical topics. Eventually, he says to me emphatically, "The reason we disagree is that you believe the Bible is inspired." I thought to myself, "of course I do…that's why I'm in seminary studying the Bible!" He went on to say, "I believe that people deep down know what is good…the Bible can help, but I believe more in the goodness of people than the Bible." He applied his belief to homosexuality, stating that if the majority of people are saying homosexuality is good, then even though the Bible holds same-sex relations as being among the many sexual sins, he doesn't believe it to be so.

I walked away from that conversation knowing what I already knew, which is this man needed to submit to the Lord. The Gospel story is predicated on the fact of God's love for human beings that are NOT naturally good. We were created to be good, but we have all been tainted by sin and as a result, we have gone astray from the Lord (Isaiah 53:6). We have rebelled against God and need to be redeemed. Jesus came to show us a better way, to show us the Kingdom, and to save us from ourselves. Hence, what this man believed was totally opposite of the Gospel. Jesus came to save sinners, not good people. We live in a world where there are murders, rapes, thefts, extortions, gossip, slander, depression, sickness, poverty, divorces, and so on —how can humanity know what's good when we create many of these problems in the world. In short, this man who was a fellow student assumed that all people are good because he never understood the necessity of the Gospel. He needs the Gospel for himself, and yet, he is a pastor today. Just because someone has a theological degree doesn't mean they know Christ.

I could spend forever on this subject but the fact of the matter is that the "Non-Christian Pastor" usually doesn't care much for the authority of the Bible or even the exclusivity of salvation found in Christ alone. These Hirelings are convinced that if a Christian assumes the Bible to be the only inspired book of God, then you are in ignorance. But this Hireling couldn't be more wrong. I feel bad for the congregation whose pastor is the "Non-Christian Pastor." Because the congregation is often left in the dark and not exposed to the light of Biblical truth. This Hireling is the definition of the "blind leading the blind."—attempting to teach the congregation about a God this Hireling doesn't know.

Grace That Promotes Sin

What matters to this Hireling the most is how relatable they are to people. They cross the line intentionally, wanting their congregation to know that they struggle like everybody else. They will intentionally cuss, drink, and smoke because they think it makes them relevant. They want people to know that they watch the same ungodly TV shows as everyone else. If this Hireling is entertained with "entertainment" where there are aggressive sex scenes and foul language throughout, then they tell their congregation, "it's just entertainment, no big deal."

This is not to say that a pastor cannot watch movies, enjoy outings, and so forth. However, when you are a Christian leader you are held to a higher standard. Yes, all Christians are held to a high standard. Nevertheless, when I read passages in 1 Timothy and Titus on Biblical eldership or Christian leadership, it is abundantly clear that Christian leaders are held to a strong standard.

A pastor should be willing to live a lifestyle that is both publicly and privately in prudence to the Lord. Pastors should always ask themselves, "If people imitated my public and private life, would they be closer to God? Or would they have a bunch of secret or public addictions and brokenness in their life?" No pastor is perfect, but if a pastor is truly practicing holiness, has a regular devotional life, and is truly saved and filled with the Spirit, then that pastor should be able to say, "Yes, people would be closer to God if they followed my example." While all Christians are to cultivate their own relationship with God, the pastor is a role model. And if a pastor is truly called of God that pastor will make the sacrifice necessary for leadership and live a holy and prudent life for one's own sake and the sake of the people the pastor is leading.

Of course, as a pastor, you are allowed to have fun, but your lifestyle shouldn't be promoting sin in other people's lives. Even if some pastors believe they can drink alcohol so long as they are not getting drunk (Proverbs 23:20a), they should still consider that perhaps there are times when they shouldn't drink, such as if it influences people negatively who cannot practice self-control with alcohol.

The Bible warns that teachers will be judged more strictly (James 3:1). Why? Because when you are in a position of influence, such as the pastor, then God will hold you responsible for what you teach and the role model you are. But this Hireling is not pursuing a godly lifestyle. Sure, they seem like nice people because they walk their neighbor's dogs, they donate to charities, and give some nice messages. But just like all the Hirelings I have mentioned, God is not approving of what they do. For this Hireling is exactly what it says in Jude:

"Dear friends, although I was very eager to write to you about the salvation we share, I felt compelled to write and urge you to contend for the faith that was once for all entrusted to God's holy people. For certain individuals whose condemnation was written about long ago have secretly slipped in among you. They are ungodly people, who pervert the grace of our God into a license for immorality and deny Jesus Christ our only Sovereign and Lord." (Jude 1:3-4)

This Hireling believes and teaches that because of God's grace you are free to sin as much as you want to. This couldn't be any further from the truth. The reality is that when you have experienced God's grace, you no longer want to sin like you used to. Of course, there are times when you struggle, but having experienced God's grace working in your life is so beautiful and powerful that you don't want to willfully sin anymore. You will never be perfect because you are not God. But you will begin to pursue Him with all your strength because now you love Him.

According to the Bible, God's grace doesn't just remove the penalty of sin and shame from your life, but it empowers you to live righteous lives: *"For the grace of God has appeared that offers salvation to all people. It teaches us to say 'No' to ungodliness and worldly passions and to live self-controlled, upright and godly lives in this present age,"* (Titus 2:11-12). Hence, as a Christian under grace, you should be growing in your sanctification and becoming more like Christ because grace empowers you to overcome your sins. Again you will not be perfect, but you will be growing.

Now let me speak directly to you, the reader. As a Christian, you don't need anybody to celebrate your sin and you don't need anybody condemning you either

(Romans 8:1). On the contrary, you need Christians in your life that you not only have fun with, but they also keep you accountable in love. More importantly, your pastor should be someone that represents grace, love, accountability, and discipline. But unfortunately, if you have this Hireling for a pastor, they want to celebrate your sin and make it seem like it's no big deal when it is. Remember sin was so serious, Jesus had to die in your place because of it.

Needs To Be Saved

The spiritual reality is that the "Non-Christian Pastor" needs to be born again—they need to be saved. Jesus made it very clear that there is coming a day, where spiritual leaders who were false will be exposed. Jesus speaking about judgement day said:

"'Not everyone who says to me, 'Lord, Lord,' will enter the kingdom of heaven, but only the one who does the will of my Father who is in heaven. Many will say to me on that day, 'Lord, Lord, did we not prophesy in your name and in your name drive out demons and in your name perform many miracles?' Then I will tell them plainly, 'I never knew you. Away from me, you evildoers.'" (Matthew 7:21-23)

Did you catch the emphasis on punishment for Christian leaders in the passage? There are going to be Christian leaders that could be youth ministers, Sunday school teachers, evangelists, elders, deacons, and pastors, who have done all these great things in the name of the Lord. And yet, Christ is going to say "I never knew you." Wow, if what I have been saying about shattered pulpits and false pastors haven't convinced you yet, this passage should. According to this passage, It is entirely possible to be extremely gifted, skillful, and even operate in supernatural gifts, and yet not be saved! You say "how can that be?" Because God gives gifts to people and they can still operate those gifts even if they aren't obedient to God, but eventually judgement day will come. God gave us the gift of intellect, sex, and creativity, and just think about how people in the world have abused just those three gifts! The intellect is a gift from God, but some people intellectualize themselves into thinking that God doesn't exist. Sex is a gift from God and was meant to be between a man and woman in marriage, but some people abuse the gift of sex in many ways. Creativity is a gift from God, but some people use their creativity to make bombs to hurt people— God didn't give us all these gifts so we could abuse them —but humanity has.

What I'm trying to say is that the "Non-Christian Pastor" may be gifted, skillful, interesting, charismatic, and intellectual; they might have all manner of gifts and say that they do it for the Lord—but the Lord they are talking about is the one they have created in their own mind. If you have a pastor like this, and they don't repent, get fired, or leave soon, then maybe you should consider leaving. Nonetheless, please pray for pastors (Hirelings) like this, they need to know the grace of our Savior and be saved.

Solving The Problem

(This section will be at the end of every chapter to remind you of this truth.)

Dear reader, it's important for you to know that the "Non-Christian Pastor" and the other pastors/Hirelings mentioned in this book can absolutely be restored! God loves all people, including the pastors who might have lost their way. If you are a Christian leader and you feel convicted as you are reading the contents of this book, then you need to know that conviction doesn't mean condemnation (Romans 8:1). God loves you and is using this book as a wake-up call for you to turn some things around.

Therefore, while this book has/will diagnose the many problems behind the pulpit, let's not write these pastors off too quickly. God has provided a way for pastors to be restored. In chapter ten, I will reveal the solution for this

pervasive problem in a section entitled, "Problem Solved."
Because of Christ, there is hope.

EIGHT

SOCIAL MEDIA PASTOR

Several years ago, I had a minister friend who got fired from his church because of an ongoing sin issue in his life that was affecting the congregation. Immediately the next month, he started going on social media and preaching to people. He decided that if he couldn't preach in front of a physical crowd, he would create a congregation on social media. And it did work. People have supported his social media outlets and are liking his messages. But the problem is that he was fired from his church because of sin. And instead of taking the proper time to heal and be renewed by God, he jumped immediately to another platform (social media) and started preaching. Basically, the person you are watching on a screen could have character issues that are hard to detect through the social media platform.

What we all discover is that getting to know someone over the phone or social media is completely different than meeting them in person. There is more you can pick up concerning a person's character when they are physically in front of you. How many times have you met someone in person and they may have either exceeded or failed to meet your expectations? It's because more was revealed when you engaged with them beyond a form of social media. When you have a local pastor, you meet their family (if they have a family), you see them around the community, you feel what it's like to be in their presence, and therefore you have a better opportunity to understand their character.

Now to be fair even a pastor that is physically present with you could be masquerading behind a persona. They could act one way at church events, in the community, and so forth; and be completely different when nobody is around. Nevertheless, there's still greater opportunity to know the pastor your talking to when you are in their presence. For example, as a pastor myself, I have to be vulnerable to my congregation. Because there isn't a screen between me and somebody in my church, I find myself able to be more humble and sincere when I'm interacting with them. These aren't just people that I can mute, ban, or unfriend from my social media channel. Absolutely not! These are real people. I scc them at church, the grocery store, the movie theater, or at my kids sporting events. There have been times when I'm outside jogging and a church member drives by and screams from their car, "PASTORRRRR BRIIIANNN." My members aren't just names scrolling on my social media channel, avatars, or short-lived video conferences. On the contrary, I will run into these people in different nondigital real-life situations. So how I treat or care for them is important—number one because I have a responsibility to God as a pastor to serve His people, and number two because I'm bound to see them in person regularly. They have an opportunity to see and sense the example of my life, and not just the content I present on a screen.

What I'm trying to say is this: Too many Christians are flocking to social media preachers because of their short (sometimes lengthy), catchy, beautifully, and graphically designed messages, without actually considering the theological framework, character, and motivation of the person on the screen. While preaching and teaching on social media isn't inherently wrong, it must be done right and in the auspices of the local church. I am a proponent of using social media to promote the message of Christ. I even have a couple of social media channels to share the Gospel message with others. I am not opposed to the proper use of it. However, there is a way to use it correctly and wrongly. And it is my assertion that the Hireling known as the "Social Media Pastor" undermines the authority of the Church as Jesus set it in order. In fact, they consciously or unconsciously cripple the faith walk of the believer. Hence, in this chapter, I'm going to do my best to explain the problems this Hireling does to the body of Christ. And hopefully, you will also see how social media for the purposes of preaching and teaching can be a great thing when done correctly.

Turns You Into A Fan

In my encounters, these Hirelings know how to talk about theology, spirituality, and practicalities in compelling ways. They are so tech savvy with their camera angles, lighting, and captions. But they are more interested in turning you into their fan than a disciple of Christ.

I've met a lot of these social media pastors, and one of the things they love to talk about the most is how many followers they have on their social media outlets. One of these types of Hirelings came into my church. And when I shook his hand and introduced myself, he immediately started talking about all his social media exploits. He compared himself to me and said, "Hey, I got a congregation too. I got about 16,000 followers on Facebook, and over a hundred more on Youtube." And that wasn't all. He was talking so fast that I forgot about the numbers on his other social media platforms. Basically, what I noticed as we were talking, or really as he was talking, is that he was more focused on the numbers than anything else. He said his preaching and teaching on social media was about Christ. And perhaps that was the content he was presenting to his "fans" but the content of his character was pride!

He never mentioned anything about people experiencing salvation, about praying for the people, about feeling the pain of the people he was ministering to, or plugging them into a local congregation where they could experience community and grow from other believers. However, the true pastors I know, that actually come in contact with physical people, talk about those important things. But this Hireling just wants you to "like," "comment," "subscribe," and "share" their social media platform with as many people as possible to increase their fame. Plus, some social media outlets can be monetized. In other words, the social media personality can make money because the more followers he or she has, means the more opportunity they have for companies to pay them to advertise on their social media.

So what's the main priority of this Hireling? Is it to make you a disciple of Jesus Christ? No, they want to make you their fan! Their online congregation is like a bunch of groupies singing their praises more than they do God. Their shattered pulpit is a camera lens in which they stand behind it acting to care for people they never intend to meet. Their social media is run like a reality show—and they love that idea—that people watch them for entertainment. I've even seen some "Christian" social media platforms where the personality or preacher who claims to be teaching people about Christ, barely says anything about Christ. They just do a live video of themselves eating potato chips and talking to random people that log in. And their fans think, "This guy is awesome." Why? Because they occasionally talk about God and give you reviews on potato chips? Why? Because you love their personality and they "liked" something you posted in the comment section? Sometimes these Hirelings present themselves in ways, hoping that some television network will turn them into the next Christian reality show. Their social media outlets become places where you do hear some things about Christ, and although they may have started with Christ as their motivation, they are now a slave to getting as many "subscribers" and "likes" as possible.

They don't want to admit it, but it's the number of "likes" that drives what they do. They're looking to create a seven-minute video or live video that produces the most "likes" and "shares" as possible. Make no mistake about it, many of these social media preachers are after the approval of people. In the deepest recesses of their being where God should have control, they have replaced it with this thought in one form or another, "If I don't get any views on this video I must not be significant to the Kingdom of God." What they don't realize is that they have already minimized their significance, because they entertain and nurture that thought over and over again.

Child of God, you need to know that you were never meant to be turned into a fan, you are supposed to be turned into a disciple of Christ. There are some good social media preachers who can help you in your faith walk towards Christ. However, a lot of them are using you to increase their fame. When Jesus came on the scene and started to have a public ministry, John the Baptist recognized that his ministry had to "decrease" so that Christ's ministry could "increase" in the public sphere (John 3:30). But this Hireling doesn't want to decrease at all. Their vanity is hidden under the guise of wanting to share the Gospel on social media. They just want to be famous and make money from it. Don't you dare become somebody's fan, child of God. A true pastor wants to help you become a disciple of Christ.

Usually No Accountability

Some of these Hirelings are not connected to a local church at all. They do not belong to a church where there are elders, deacons, and other members of the church to keep them accountable (Philippians 1:1, Hebrews 13:17). I have had one of these Hirelings say they belonged to a church I was serving at the time. He came maybe three times consistently, and then he started showing up maybe once every four to six months. He wasn't really a part of our church, but whenever he would show up maybe three times a year, he would say I was his pastor and how he was inviting people to the church. One time I watched some of his teachings on his social media platform and at one point in the live video, he told people they should belong to a church. He even mentioned my church saying that he was a member. I immediately started laughing because he didn't belong to a church. Basically, he would pop up at my church a few times a year just to tell people he was going to church. So what was he doing? He was being hypocritical on social media by telling people to attend church and he was also using my church to give himself credibility by making it seem like he regularly attended as well.

Regardless of what people say a Christian should belong to a local church where there is a physically present pastor and other congregation members to love and challenge them to higher levels in their Christian faith. I know in the 21st century it has become a popular notion that you don't have to go to church to be a Christian, and that's true. However, because you are a Christian, you should want to belong to a church.

Football players want to belong to a team, lawyers want to belong to a firm, cinema lovers go to theaters, dancers find places to dance, foodies go out to restaurants, runners will run with other runners. Typically, people look for a community to join that have the same interests. And when you are a part of a group you experience more joy seeing people doing the things you enjoy. Moreover, the group helps you be accountable so that you can experience success in what the group collectively enjoys.

For example, even at the movie theater, there is accountability which produces more joy for everyone. You could stay at home and watch a movie, but there's something that makes a movie even funnier when others are laughing at it with you. The movie becomes even more epic when not only you but others in the theater gasp for air at what they just saw. And you're even expected to practice a type of social etiquette at the theater (E.g., no talking, silence your cell phone, etc.). When everybody is enjoying the same movie and people feel accountable to one another by showing respect and not distracting people from the movie, people walk away having a better experience than what they could have gotten at home alone.

Likewise, when we gather as the body of Christ, and the Spirit of God is sensed, we feel accountable to one another, we experience God in such a mighty way that it empowers us to live our lives for Christ until we meet again! Unfortunately, you might not know what it's like to have a Spirit-led service if you have one of these Hirelings like the "Rigid Theologian Pastor" we previously talked about who doesn't believe in the power of the Spirit. Nonetheless, this is how a church should be. The church is a luxury and a beautiful community that we should be looking forward to every week.

There is so much to be gained from being physically present at a local church with other believers. You may say you love other believers, but you don't really know that until you go to church and sit next to other believers that might have hang-ups and attitude problems like you occasionally do—can you love other Christians that have broken moments like you or would you just rather stay home and avoid them? If you don't want to be around other Christians right now then why go to Heaven? There's going to be a lot of Christians there!

The Bible makes it clear that we should want to be around other believers and that our love for other believers demonstrates that we are disciples (Hebrews 10:25, John 13:34-35). In essence, you cannot love God if you do not love His people (1 John 4:20). Yes, you can cheer for your favorite "Social Media Pastor," while wearing your pajamas at home. However, will you show your other brothers and sisters in Christ that you love them, by being willing to meet with them at church?

What I'm trying to say is that this Hireling helps reinforce the idea that "I don't have to go to church to be a Christian." Due to the fact that this Hireling bounces from one random church to the next just to be able to say they "go" to church, but with no real commitment, this Hireling in effect will turn you into a reflection of themselves. As you continue to feed their ego by watching their videos, they turn you into a lazy Christian, in which you think your Christianity is all about you. Because of this Hireling's influence, you don't want to belong to a church, you don't give financially, physically, or spiritually to a church or attempt to reach lost people. You think Christianity is just about consuming as much content as your "Social Media Pastor" produces. You limit evangelism to "sharing" their video to others because you are their fan. But when you are a disciple you should be learning to do evangelism yourself. You get high on their content and become spiritually fat with all that you have consumed from this Hireling's social media platform. But they typically have no accountability to a church and usually the people who follow this Hireling also feel like they don't have to be accountable to a church. Again, there is a positive side to using social media for ministry that I will explain at the end of this chapter.

Doesn't Care For You Personally

How rare would it be for a strictly social media preacher to do a funeral for your loved one that just passed away? The social media preacher you love the most could possibly be as close as several miles away from you or live on another continent. The reality is when a family member dies or if you were to pass away, you would want a local pastor who was truly involved in your life to do the funeral. While you may love what the "Social Media Pastor" produces over the internet, there's a strong chance that person is not coming to do a funeral for you.

Once more, I remember talking to one of these Hirelings at a church, and he told me how some of his "followers" have requested his presence. He claimed that one of his followers had been sick and wanted him to come by for prayer. He then said to me, "That's not me! I can't visit people." And I thought to myself, "of course you can't… they are just your fans, you are not really their pastor." Now a local pastor cannot make every visit either. Nonetheless, the typical church usually trains deacons or elders to visit members when the pastor can't. But this Hireling doesn't have any intention of visiting because they are just a social media personality. Even if they did show up to your house for a visit, they would have to do a live video recording of it so all their other fans would see how awesome they are.

This is where a local pastor really outshines this Hireling. Your local pastor may have actually been a part of your life in multiple ways. And it's the local pastor that should want to do your funeral. The local pastor is the one that has been praying for you specifically. The local pastor is the one that has been trying to train you in practical ways to serve other Christians and the community. Christians should be a part of a local church, where they have a pastor and others that actually care about them.

The Proper Function Of Social Media Ministry

Okay, I'm sorry if I have come across really harsh about social media ministry because I actually love it. People just need to understand the problems with it. So here is what you have been waiting to hear: There is a great aspect to using social media to deliver dynamic, compelling, Biblical, and spirit filed messages to the masses. The internet and social media excite me about the possibilities of being able to share Christ with the world. Imagine a situation where someone is thinking about suicide or using the internet to look up pornography, but they stumble upon a social media preacher and it dramatically stops them from doing something detrimental. What if somebody watches a social media preacher clearly explain the Gospel in a way that causes the person watching, to submit their life to Christ and find a local church where their faith can be nurtured? Just the thought of these events happening makes me overjoyed as someone who wants to see the Gospel reach the world.

I believe a "Social Media Pastor" can be a celebrated minister so long as they have the covering and support of a local church, where they are accountable to church leadership and other believers who can vouch for their character and make sure they are Biblically sound. I believe social media pastors can be supplemental to a person's faith walk but should not replace the local pastor and the local church. I even know of some really good local pastors who will use social media to reach people. There's one pastor I watch on social media, and at the very beginning of every message he does, he reminds people that they should be a participant of a local church. He has a lot of "subscribers" but he implores all of them to get into a local church and not just watch his videos—that's a good way to use social media.

The bottom line is that if you are a Christian trying to avoid church or you're bashing the Church, you are wrong. Yes, God still loves you, but you're wrong. Jesus made a great statement, He said, *"...I will build my church, and the gates of Hades will not overcome it,"* (Matthew 16:18). Based on this Scripture it seems to me that Jesus loves the Church. And yes, there may be some fake and ungodly churches out there. If there are fake pastors then there must also be fake churches that Jesus never established. Nonetheless, according to this Scripture, there are churches out there and "hades" or "hell" is not overcoming them. So if you refuse to belong to a church, because you think they're all hypocritical or fake, then you are saying Jesus is wrong. There are churches that have been established by Christ, you need to belong to the one God has called you!

Thank God for the "Social Media Pastor" that is truly serving God without undermining His people and His Church. Yes, I hope people "like" and "share" videos of social media preachers who actually produce Biblically sound content and belong to a local church. However, if you are the Hireling that is using social media to build your fame and if you are turning God's people into your fans instead of the Lord's disciples, I'm praying for you to change. I pray you would repent to God and ask for forgiveness from your fans on your social media outlets. And lastly, I want to say to this Hireling, before you just tell people to like, subscribe, and share your channel, perhaps you should at some point tell them to belong to a church.

Solving The Problem

(This section will be at the end of every chapter to remind you of this truth.)

Dear reader, it's important for you to know that the "Social Media Pastor" and the other pastors/Hirelings mentioned in this book can absolutely be restored! God loves all people, including the pastors who might have lost their way. If you are a Christian leader and you feel convicted as you are reading the contents of this book, then you need to know that conviction doesn't mean condemnation

(Romans 8:1). God loves you and is using this book as a wake-up call for you to turn some things around.

Therefore, while this book has/will diagnose the many problems behind the pulpit, let's not write these pastors off too quickly. God has provided a way for pastors to be restored. In chapter ten, I will reveal the solution for this pervasive problem in a section entitled, "Problem Solved." Because of Christ, there is hope.

NINE

KINGDOM-MINDED PASTOR

We have spent considerable time identifying the shattered pulpits of these debunked Hirelings who all have been bought for a price. And now it's time to identify the real pastors. Throughout this book, you have heard me reference to good pastors by identifying them as "true" or "real" pastors. Well, every true and real pastor is a "Kingdom-minded Pastor." While an entire book could be written about the "Kingdom-minded Pastor," this chapter is just going to touch on a few highlights. Nonetheless, it should be extensive enough for you to know a "Kingdom-minded Pastor" when you are around one.

The "Kingdom-minded Pastor" is focused on the Kingdom of God. They live and enjoy certain things in this world, but their source of identity from which they always draw is being a Kingdom citizen. They live within the boundaries, regulations, and governing bodies of the world, while simultaneously serving an even greater Kingdom. They know that any democracy, monarchy, or dictatorship of the world cannot compare to the theocracy of following Christ.

When the Kingdom is present, the true preaching of the Gospel will happen (Matthew 24:14). Not the social justice, moralistic, or prosperity Gospel—those would be different subjects; but the Gospel of Jesus Christ in which men and women are saved from the wrath of a Holy God and are transformed into Kingdom citizens because of Christ's sacrifice. According to John the Baptist repentance happens when the Kingdom of God is present (Matt 3:2). People will begin to confess their sins, repent of their sins, and follow Jesus. The demonstration of the supernatural happens. As Jesus proclaimed the Kingdom of God was near He also healed many (Matthew 4:23-25). The casting out of demons is evidence of the Kingdom (Luke 11:20), that God's power is greater than the kingdom of darkness. The Apostles preached about the Kingdom of God (Acts 19:8). Jesus talked about what life in the Kingdom looked like (Matthew 5:1-7:27). This is all to say, the Kingdom of God is the expressed culture that comes with norms, ethics, morality, power, and authority.

The Kingdom of God counteracts the effects of a sinful world; it displays an even greater existence than what we have experienced. For example, when John the Baptist struggled to believe the Kingdom of God was near, Jesus sent messengers to tell Him evidence of the Kingdom. Jesus said, *"'Go back and report to John what you have seen and heard: The blind receive sight, the lame walk, those who have leprosy are cleansed, the deaf hear, the dead are raised, and the good news is proclaimed to the poor. Blessed is anyone who does not stumble on account of me,'"* (Luke 7:22-23).

In short, the "Kingdom-minded Pastor" totally embraces their citizenship as belonging to the Kingdom of God. When they deal with issues of the world, they don't do so as a conservative or liberal, as a political party, as a race or gender, as these Hirelings are in the habit of doing. But rather, Kingdom-minded pastors know they belong to God. The "Kingdom-minded Pastor" represents the Kingdom of God and in every ministry endeavor, they have this mentality. The "Kingdom-minded Pastor" is better than a Pentecostal, Baptist, Methodist, Presbyterian, Lutheran, or any other denomination or association you can think of. These denominations would adamantly disagree, and many denominations may have started with noble intentions, but now they have agendas that aren't Biblical or reflective of the Kingdom. However, the Kingdom-minded Pastor's theological framework, pursuits, and lifestyle (both public and private) screams the Kingdom of God. They aren't trying to impress some denominational/associational figurehead; they aren't worried about keeping up with what the world wants to talk about; they are consumed by God. If a pastor is truly called by God, they will have a Kingdom mindset. This pastor does not have a shattered pulpit because they are truly operating in the will of God. This one chapter will not do this pastor justice. I only hope it gives you some insight on who the pastor is really called to be.

Revealing Traits

The "Kingdom-minded Pastor" always has these revealing qualities:

Calling: This type of person became a pastor because they were actually called by God. The Hireling will take a church "job" because of the desired location, skill set, salary, and prominence of the position. They take church "jobs" because of their own will. However, the "Kingdom-minded Pastor" goes exactly where God tells them to go. Samuel became a prophet because God called him to be a prophet (1 Samuel 3:1-10), not because he had the best resume out of the bunch, a required degree or reached a certain age. God anoints and supports the "Kingdom-minded Pastor," but not the Hireling.

Character: Their character is fit for the task at hand. It doesn't mean they are perfect, but they are pursuing a holy and righteous life. They know that their Christian lifestyle and ministry is highly dependent upon the Holy Spirit, so they spend time in prayer. They are in the presence of God regularly, and their character reflects that. What makes their character so sharp and brilliant is because everything they do is for God. Most Christians say they are doing everything for God, but this pastor means it—they really believe that how they treat people including themselves is a reflection of how they would treat God. They have integrity because they know that one day they will stand before God for every sermon, counsel, how they handled church finances, and so forth. They are not afraid to look at their faults and make amends where they can. David had a great character, and when he had sinned he confessed his sins before God (Psalm 51). Just like David, the "Kingdom-minded Pastor" won't pretend like their sin doesn't exist. They will confess, repent, receive forgiveness, and become stronger in their faith.

Commitment: Because they are assured they heard the voice of God concerning the calling, they will be committed to it. Whatever ministry God has called them to, they will want to please God in it. The Hireling is only committed so long as it serves selfish ambition—when things get too tough the Hireling will abandon the congregation or mission. However, people like Elijah, Mary, Gideon, and the like didn't give up. They may have had some struggles but they were committed. The Hireling will quit when things get beyond their control, but not so with the Kingdom pastor who buckles down, digs their heels in and in effect says, "I am going to bring glory to my God regardless of the situation." The "Kingdom-minded Pastor" truly believes that if God called them to it, God will also help them through it. They also always have a spiritual mentor/father/mother to help direct them, like how Paul was to Timothy or Elijah was to Elisha. They understand their commitment to God will be bolstered by having a mentor. They will not be isolated like the "Wounded Pastor."

Confidence: The "Kingdom-minded Pastor" is extremely confident in God! They know they are loved by God which gives them great confidence. The "Kingdom-minded Pastor" understands full well what Peter meant when he said, *"Though you have not seen him [Jesus], you love him; and even though you do not see him now, you believe in him and are filled with an inexpressible and glorious joy,"* (1 Peter 1:8). The Hireling has confidence in their skills, connections, and/or money; so if they find themselves in a situation when none of those things helps them, then they lose confidence. The "Kingdom-minded Pastor" may not be the most talented or popular, but so long as they have God, they know they will be victorious —Goliath will fall.

Scholarly And Supernatural

A "Kingdom-minded Pastor" operates both scholarly and supernaturally. I love the transformational story of the Apostle Paul. Before he became a Christ follower and an Apostle, he was a Pharisee by the name of Saul. As a Pharisee, he was very intelligent. He had to memorize lengthy parts of the Scriptures and interpret the Law of Moses for Judaism. So he had some scholarship. And when he was saved and transformed by the power of Christ, he became known as Paul. He started casting out demons, healing the sick, and talking about a variety of spiritual gifts. His scholarly and studious background as Saul aided him to argue intelligently the truths of Christ when he was on Mars Hill representing Christ as the Apostle Paul (Acts 17:22-31). And his education clearly helped his articulation of the Christian faith in the book of Romans, and really in all his writings. But he also had the power of the Holy Spirit working in his life to perform signs and wonders. Paul was so full of the power of the Spirit that people were getting healed just from touching handkerchiefs that had passed from his hands to others (Acts 19:11-12).

Some people try to make Paul completely heady and theological as if all he cared about is discussing theological concepts, structures, and principles. And some try to make him seem like he was just a radical charismatic, operating in signs and wonders without much regard for scholarship. But the reality is that he practiced both the scholarly and supernatural as a minister because he was Kingdom-minded. Even Jesus was studious. In Luke's gospel, it claims that Jesus was learning (2:40-52). And yet, Jesus was also supernatural with the most glaring and glorious example being the resurrection!

The "Kingdom-minded Pastor" understands that both scholarship and the supernatural are gifts from God. So they wield both like a sword. They are ready to give intelligent answers using their native words, and at other times they understand that the only language that will help is to use Heavenly words (tongues). They can refer you to some great theological book for your study, but they also know when they need to refer you to the power of the Holy Spirit. They prepare great messages through study and prayer, but they also know that at any time while delivering a message the Holy Spirit might have them say something they didn't plan on saying. The "Kingdom-minded Pastor" is exactly the way God wanted His pastors to be, both scholarly and supernatural.

Ambassadors

When the Hireling operates in their counterfeit role of pastor, they do so based on their insecurities, denominational/associational structure and demands, and/or comfort zones. In other words, there is another force driving what they are doing. But the "Kingdom-minded Pastor" operates knowing full well who they represent! They realize that they are representing the King of kings, Lord of lords, the Cornerstone, the Messiah, the Good Shepherd, the Great High Priest, the Lamb of God, the

Lion of Judah, the Root and Offspring of David, the Great "I Am."

The Hireling gets behind their shattered pulpit and represents every agenda under the sun. A racial agenda, gender agenda, political party agenda, self-preservation agenda, "I want to be liked agenda," and so on—they trick people into believing they represent the Kingdom of God but they are liars! They are more focused on pleasing a worldly agenda, than a Heavenly one. But when the "Kingdom-minded Pastor" comes to the forefront, they don't preach, teach, or lead from fear of people. They aren't insecure in what God has called them to be and do. They are representing God in humility and boldness. They are constantly praying for God's Kingdom to be established on the earth. They except the fact that there is an unseen spiritual world in which angels and demons are present. They see themselves as ambassadors for God and their churches are embassies that represent the ideals, norms, principles, and culture of their native land with God.

When Elijah confronted King Ahab, when David confronted Goliath, when Moses confronted the Pharaoh, when Samson confronted the Philistines, when Nehemiah confronted Sanballat, when Esther made a request to the king, when Deborah told Barak to go into battle, they all did so while representing the ideals, principles, and culture of the Kingdom of God. Likewise, the "Kingdom-minded Pastor" is unwavering in their intelligent, Biblical, and Spirit-empowered approach to the congregation, community, and the world. Hallelujah! God's leading men and women in the Bible, confronted kings and queens, principalities, and rulers; they were valiant and regal as ambassadors for the Kingdom of God! Jesus is going to return, and the "Kingdom-minded Pastor" is preparing for His return, by establishing His Kingdom in the hearts and minds of the people around them. A "Kingdom-minded Pastor" is constantly declaring that the "Kingdom of God is near."

Leads From Inspiration

The "Kingdom-minded Pastor" is truly listening to the Holy Spirit. They are asking God what to do, where to do it, and how to do what God wants. They believe in having a strategy, so long as it comes from God. Often, what they do is original because they got it from an unlimited and creative God. They guide, direct, preach, teach, and organize with the inspiration of the Holy Spirit.

The Hireling does a lot of things in their own strength, and then later claims it was faith. But the reality is that they were going to do what they wanted to do with or without God. They just have a business/ministry scheme they imagined or copied from some other ministry and they are hoping it works for them too. However, the "Kingdom-minded Pastor" thinks to themselves over and over again, "Did God really tell me to do this...because I'm not interested if God is not involved?" We see this sentiment in David's life. There was an army approaching to attack David because he was anointed King of Israel. And David seeks the Lord first before going out to fight the Philistine army. Once David gets the "go ahead" from God in prayer, then he goes out to fight his enemy because he knows God is supporting him (2 Samuel 5:17-25). Like David, the "Kingdom-minded Pastor" follows the instruction of the Lord.

However, to their discredit, the Hireling doesn't care if the Lord has said "yes" or "no," because they believe their plan is foolproof. And even if they are successful with their own plans, God will not accept their ministry attempt as praise, because they did it for their own vanity. The Hireling's lack of faith doesn't allow them to believe that God can really speak to you. "Of course God speaks or guides us from His Word, but He doesn't speak to us directly like he did to Moses or Peter," they think. On the contrary, the "Kingdom-minded Pastor" or Christian knows that God speaks directly to them without contradicting the written Word.

I remember when I was in college, being a part of a scholarship program. It was a program for students who had a commitment to developing strong character and changing the world around them. One night we gathered at our advisor's home. I was sitting at a table when I saw one of my fellow members enter the front door. He was smiling and laughing as if everything was fine when he came in the house. However, as I looked at him, I could sense the Lord telling me something was wrong with him. So I began to focus and ask the Lord quietly what was wrong. I then saw an image/vision in my mind of him sitting on his bed in his dorm room, with his hands covering his head in despair. And then I heard one word pop into my mind: "Relief."

So I approached this guy at the end of the scheduled program and I said, "This may sound a little weird…but I was praying for you and I had an image of you in your dorm room depressed, and God wanted me to tell you that He's going to bring relief to your situation." I was really nervous when I said this because he didn't look like he was in despair when he walked in. Nonetheless, he responded and said, "Oh my goodness…this morning I was talking to my mother over the phone in my dorm room, and I was upset because I felt like I was overwhelmed with work and school. My mother prayed for me and told me not to worry because God would bring me 'relief.'" He was surprised because God revealed to me his state of being in despair and had me say the same word "relief," as his mother did. Needless to say, he got out of his despair that night.

Now it's important to notice that nothing I did contradicted the Scripture. In fact, it was actually what the Holy Spirit did that night, I was just available to be used by the Holy Spirit. It was the Holy Spirit that told Philip to go share his faith with the Ethiopian eunuch (Acts 8:29-35). And Philip was just obedient to the Holy Spirit. And it was the Holy Spirit that told me to share a word of encouragement to that guy on that night. And now, as a pastor, God guides and directs me on how to lead His church. God truly does speak and guide the "Kingdom-minded Pastor" because they are available to it. They are inspired by the Holy Spirit.

They Are Violent

Let me make a statement that unfortunately isn't associated with many pastors today: Your pastor should be violent! The adjectives that most people use to describe their pastor is "nice," "cool," "good," "caring," "dynamic," and the like. It's not that these are bad adjectives, certainly, the "Kingdom-minded Pastor" can be those things, but they are much more. What about adjectives like "bold," "courageous," "faithful," and "fearless?" A true pastor is not just known for being kind, loving, and charismatic, but for being a violent person of faith.

The "Kingdom-minded Pastor" is forcefully advancing the Kingdom of God in the world. The Hireling believes their connections to prominent secular people and flattery will make things happen. Not so with the true pastor. They know that their greatest and only source is through the Holy Spirit, prayer, other believers, and the Bible. There are many Hirelings behind their shattered pulpits who have not even read the entire Bible, are allergic to prayer and fasting, and quit when things get hard. However, the "Kingdom-minded Pastor" doesn't have a plan "B." They strongly desire to be the pastors God has called them to be. It's not that they don't make mistakes or choices that lead to sin (Romans 3:23), they just aren't making excuses for it. They are growing in their sanctification and they love it. They pursue holiness and righteousness as a necessity for life and not a chore. They are over-comers, fighters, and warriors for God's Kingdom. While there are so many casual, commercialized, posing, status-quo, flattering, more focused on being a celebrity, debunked Hirelings out there, this real pastor is a breath of fresh air. Because you can actually sense the Spirit on the true pastor. They don't come across as a salesman who wants your business or is hiding a conservative or liberal political agenda behind their status as a pastor.

The true pastors are so devastating and violent to the kingdom of darkness that demons know their names:

"Some Jews who went around driving out evil spirits tried to invoke the name of the Lord Jesus over those who were demon-possessed. They would say, "In the name of the Jesus whom Paul preaches, I command you to come out."

Seven sons of Sceva, a Jewish chief priest, were doing this. One day the evil spirit answered them, "Jesus I know, and Paul I know about, but who are you?" Then the man who had the evil spirit jumped on them and overpowered them all. He gave them such a beating that they ran out of the house naked and bleeding." (Acts 19:13-16)

The Hirelings in the passage thought they could cast out demons like the Apostle Paul, and got their pants literally beat off of them—demons had no respect for the Hirelings back then or now. However, those demons knew who Paul was. They knew he was a Kingdom man who was not to be trifled with. The "Kingdom-minded Pastor" lives their life in such a way, both publicly and secretly, that they have a reputation with demons. When Demons see this pastor they say, "Oh no...this one actually believes in the power of prayer; oh no, this one actually operates in the anointing of God; oh no, this one is actually producing the fruit of the Spirit; oh no, this one has a faith that is contagious; oh no, this one is actually listening and following the plans of God, oh no, this one is not intimidated by us!"

In short, Jesus talked about having a violent faith (Matthew 11:12), and this pastor has it. It's not that they are free of mistakes or haven't staggered in their faith, they just don't have a price and thus, have not been bought like the Hirelings. The "Kingdom-minded Pastor" is full of humility, grace, tenacity, and resolve for the Kingdom of God. Thank you, God, for the real pastors who are shining examples.

Getting Beyond The Pastor

In this book, we have said a lot about the "pastor." Who the pastor is and who the pastor is not. However, the "Kingdom-minded Pastor" may not actually be a pastor. They could be an Apostle, Prophet, Evangelist, or Teacher (Ephesians 4:11-16). You could be reading this book as a deacon, elder, or Sunday school teacher. Or perhaps, you might not recognize your spiritual gift or the ministry you are called to just yet, but you are a Christian. Whoever you are, the Christian life is meant to be about the Kingdom of God. While this book has been addressing the position or office of "pastor" I have prayed that this book would speak to all Christians. I pray that you would evaluate your own life and ask the question, "Lord, in what ways have I acted like a Hireling?" In other words, have there been areas in your Christian life in which you have been bought or compromised? God loves you. We can always repent to a loving Savior.

I pray for all you Kingdom pastors/leaders out there. Some of you don't get acknowledged for your sacrifice but God celebrates you. Some of you have been rejected and despised because you stand up for godly principles, but God has accepted you. Some of you have had people lie about your character, but God knows the truth. Keep on establishing the Kingdom of God in the area to which He has called you. After all, one day God is going to acknowledge you with a crown on your head (James 1:12).

TEN

SHOULD YOUR PASTOR BE FIRED?

Obviously, the subtitle of this book, "Should Your Pastor Be Fired?" suggests that some pastors should be removed from their positions of authority. That is exactly what I mean because there are far too many Hirelings behind pulpits today. For those Hirelings out there that are hell-bent and committed to corrupting and hurting God's people by what they say and do, shame on you. Your day to stand before a Holy God will come. You who prostitute, use, abuse, and corrupt God's people, I pray that you would be ousted from the pulpit quickly. I pray that every false pastor/Christian leader in America and abroad who refuses to repent would be removed. Too many pastors have become pastors because of ulterior motives apart from God. Moreover, it's important to understand that the majority of these Hirelings mentioned in this book didn't start out as a Hireling. In truth, some people have become pastors without having ill intentions, but they just didn't know any better. In the following are a couple of reasons of how people ignorantly become pastors:

Spiritual Maturity: Some people mature in their faith and they think that they are ready for a new spiritual challenge. Hence, this person thinks that by becoming a pastor, they will be able to help more people. This person was not called by God, and they probably would have done better serving under a called pastor at a local congregation. In other words, this person could have fulfilled another ministry role and had a significant impact at a church as a Bible study leader, youth minister, outreach coordinator, etc., but in their mind, the only way to do ministry and demonstrate maturity as a disciple was to become a pastor.

Family Lineage: You have met the pastor that said, "I come from a family of ministers/pastors." However, just because someone's great-grandfather, cousins, and so forth, were pastors, does not mean this person is called.

People, like the above mentioned, become pastors many times because they have a "good idea" but not a "God idea." They became pastors because their history, connections, and good intentions made it seem advantageous. They get behind a pulpit perhaps with some savvy and skills, and yet God is not supporting their ministry because it was their "good idea," not God's. And because God never called them, and there is no anointing behind what they do—indeed, they have a shattered pulpit.

Disqualified

Still, others may have started well (God actually called them) but they finish poorly because sin corrupts them. We see this take place with King Saul. God called him to be the King of Israel (1 Samuel 9:15-17). And he did well until his fear and pride got the best of him. Saul was Israel's king but in worry, he tried to act like the priest/prophet Samuel. Only a priest was allowed to make a sacrifice to God on behalf of God's people. But Saul was in the middle of a war and was outnumbered and the priest —Samuel—was late. So wanting to win the war, Saul thinks, "I'll make the sacrifice in Samuel's stead, and gain God's favor." Shortly, after Saul makes the sacrifice, Samuel shows up and tells Saul that because he acted out of place, God was stripping the kingdom from him and giving it to another who would be David (1 Samuel 13:5-14)

Just like King Saul, a pastor may have started out called and anointed by God, but they get dominated by an unconfessed and unrepented sin. Sure, even called pastors can and do sin, but they are willing to confess it, repent of it, and step down from their position if necessary to get whole again. However, if a pastor entertains sin continually and/or purposely…let's say a pastor has a porn addiction, abuses substances, or has a bully mentality, then those pastors disqualify themselves (1 Corinthians 9:27).

The pastor may have once been called by God, but they allowed sin to dominate their life. Therefore, they still may be talented but they have a shattered pulpit. God has removed His anointing/approval of them and they should be fired.

Sent By Demons

Furthermore, some pastors weasel into a church with malicious intent from the beginning. They are sent by demons and have every intention of harming God's people. They are not thinking about the state of someone's soul and making them Kingdom citizens, they are focused on what they want. They steal money from the church, have relations with different members, turn the house of God into a business, and pervert the truth. Needless to say, this type of pastor should be fired.

Fired Up

In one sense this book has identified the many Hirelings that should be fired. And that is one way to look at the subtitle of this book. Because not only do I mean "Should Your Pastor Be Fired?," as in removed, but I also mean "Should Your Pastor Be Fired Up?" Your pastor should absolutely be on fire for the Kingdom of God. We need

Kingdom-minded pastors that are prayerful, faithful, passionate, and tenacious.

Before going any further, it needs to be said that pastors do experience hardships and although they should be burning up for God, they might have moments in which they feel burnt out. I don't want to give the impression that being in the service of God is easy or as if real pastors don't ever feel overwhelmed. The prophet Elijah indeed was a man on fire for God. He defied the prophets of Baal with fire, he went up to heaven to meet God in a chariot of fire, God is a consuming fire, and Elijah, without a doubt, reflected that in his ministry. Nonetheless, we did see a moment in which he felt burnt out.

One would think that after Elijah defeated the prophets of Baal in the style he did, he would be elated and have nothing to fear. However, when queen Jezebel discovers that Elijah killed her prophets of Baal she sends word to Elijah that she wants him dead. Shockingly, Elijah—who is usually bold and anointed—runs for his life because he feared the threat of Jezebel. Elijah found himself sitting under a tree depressed, tired, wanting to die, and eventually he hides in a cave (1 Kings 19:1-9). The pressure had become so much for him that he no longer wanted to exist.

As he's in the cave mourning for his life, he told God that he was the only prophet left, the only faithful person. He believed this until God told him, *"'Yet I reserve seven thousand in Israel—all whose knees have not bowed down to Baal and whose mouths have not kissed him,'"* (1 Kings 19:18). Elijah became burnt out for a moment in his ministry because he let fear take his focus off of God, and he felt like nobody else was supporting him. But God reminded him that He was there for him, and there were still thousands of faithful people in Israel just like Elijah!

Elijah's biggest hang up is that he felt like he didn't have any support. Dear reader, if you really believe pastors should be fired up for the things of God, then please support them. You can absolutely support other ministries or pastors outside of your local church that are truly called by God. However, you really need to support your local pastor! Your local pastor is the one that is really praying for you, knows your story, has been equipping you, and while your pastor does this as a servant of the Lord, it would help if you believed, contributed to, or supported your local pastor as much as you do a famous preacher on TV or social media.

This is not to say that a famous preacher is inherently evil, no of course not, John the Baptist, the Apostle Paul, and Jesus were famous preachers. But what I am saying is that some of you may have some incredible and anointed local pastors, but you spend more time praying for, listening to, contributing financially towards, and "sharing" the media outlets of your favorite social media pastors and their ministry. Meanwhile, the local pastor who might be just as gifted as your favorite social media/television ministry doesn't get your support. What I am saying is this: Do not let a great local pastor experience burnout because you, as members of the church, don't support the ministry. Some people will drive hours to listen to, serve, and give financially to a ministry conference of a famous pastor or Christian speaker (I have done this). Nonetheless, do not forget that your local church and its pastors have been given a mission from God. And if you are really a part of the church you go to, your pastor should be able to inspire you to contribute spiritually, financially, and physically to the church and local mission.

Even though a pastor may experience burnout if they feel like they are not supported, the truth of the matter is that every "Kingdom-minded Pastor" doesn't have to experience burnout. It happens, but the Scripture gives great promises that will keep the real pastor from burning out including this one: *"You will keep in perfect peace those whose minds are steadfast, because they trust in you,"* (Isaiah 26:3). Your pastor should be fired up. Let's fan the flame of those pastors and Christian leaders called by God by supporting them.

Don't Become A Hammer

While this book has been used as a tool to expose the Hirelings behind pulpits today, I want to make it explicitly clear that this book should not be used as a hammer. In other words, we should be discerning what is of God and what is not, but by no means should you be running around like the pulpit police and be condemning every pastor you see (you might need to reread chapter one in the section subtitled "Discernment" to recall what I mean).

The fact of the matter is that every one of these Hirelings named in this book can be redeemed by God if they are willing. For we know that while in leadership Peter denied Christ three times, David committed adultery and murdered a man, and Samson slept around with a lot of women, but they were all redeemed. We should never condone any sin, but we need to be careful not to assume that just because a pastor's pulpit has become shattered that they are beyond the point of return. God will expose the Hireling, but we should hope that they confess, repent, make restitution where necessary, and become what God has called them to be.

Therefore, I warn you that should you believe your pastor or a pastor has a shattered pulpit, you shouldn't make snap judgments. You should not be running around and whispering (gossiping) about the pastor whom you have concerns about. There is a Biblical process for bringing up your concerns (Matthew 18:15-17). Basically, each church is different but there should be a protocol at every church for dealing with disputes. There should be proper channels of leadership or authority for you to talk to, instead of taking it upon yourself and slandering a pastor. Be careful because you run the potential of becoming like a Judas if you judge the pastor without having all the facts. God loves the pastor you have concerns for, so I hope you treat the pastor as someone God loves. Nobody wants to be gossiped about or have people making assumptions about them. Hence, make sure you do the right thing. It is best to ask yourself the question: "Am I broaching this subject out of love or am I acting like Judas?"

Problem Solved

If you are a pastor/Christian leader reading this book, and you have recognized areas in the past or present where you were like the Hirelings mentioned (I certainly did), then you need to remember the simple truth: God loves you. We are under the dispensation of grace, and the very fact that you are reading this book tells me, there's still time. There is time through the grace of God to exchange your will for God's will and to be the "Kingdom-minded Pastor" or Christian leader you are supposed to be.

So let me share with you the age-old solution for this problem because there is hope. You may already know it but you just need to be reminded of it! Are you ready? Here is the solution: Christ has made provision for you to repent, confess, be forgiven, and continue on in the grace of God! In my book, "Wake Up Ladies," I break down this redemptive process in the following:

Repentance: This is a word that means to turn away from something that harms you, and run towards wholeness. It means to turn away from your sin and toward a loving God. And in relation to our topic, you must turn away from your ways that have perpetuated the issue. You might have to right any wrongs (words, actions, or lack thereof); turn back to God.

Confession: This is about specifically owning the ways in which you have fallen short as God's [pastor]. How have you lowered the standard for yourself or other [pastors]? At what times did you slip into passivity where you did not speak up, or how have you participated in the [sin]? Confess in prayer to God, and perhaps with others.

Forgiveness: Ask God to forgive you for whatever it is that you confessed. God is always willing to forgive us (1 John 1:9). And maybe God might lead you to ask others for their forgiveness.

Grace: Now you need to live in God's grace because you are powerless without it. God's grace not only removes your sin, but it empowers you to live the virtuous life (Romans 6:14). (110)

Even after some of you pastors/Christian leaders go through this redemptive process there are four things I want to suggest/prescribe for you:

Time off: The reason some of you pastors got into this situation is because you have not been taking a sabbath. You have burned yourself out and you need some time off to rejuvenate. Talk to your church or the powers that be about taking some time off for yourself to reconnect with God. You might even need to establish other leaders in the church to take some of the burdens off of you.

Spiritual Fathers/mentors: If you don't have other pastors or spiritual leaders in your life to help guide you, then that is a problem. Some pastors have this by formality, but they don't truly have somebody they can trust and confide in. Or, you may not have a mentor in your life due to ignorance or stubbornness. However, you need people in your life not to control you, but to help you on your journey to becoming more like Christ, not only in your leadership but in other aspects.

Prayer life: You must have a strong prayer life. And I'm not just talking about praying for your ministry. No! You need a regular prayer life in which you simply enjoy being in God's presence. Sometimes pastors get so wrapped up in preparing sermons, visiting, strategizing, and praying for others that they forget to spend time in prayer for themselves. Your prayer life will sustain you and keep you on the right track.

Read Scripture: Make sure you are nourished by the Word of God. Don't let the Bible just become the thing you read in preparation for sermons, developing Bible studies, or providing counsel. Do you remember the time where you just enjoyed reading God's Word for yourself? God will comfort and speak to you through His Word.

Deliverance: While you may be a believer who is the possession of the Lord and have a great inheritance in Christ, you could be under the oppression of a demon that needs to be casted away from your life—a demonic influence that is hindering you from God's best. Contact your spiritual father/mentor or you may need to find a minister that will do a deliverance session with you. Remember, even Peter was influenced by the Devil at one point and the Lord rebuked it, (Matthew 16:23)!

There it is! This is the solution. I want to tell every pastor or Christian leader out there not to give up. Ministry can be tough, it is tough, but God is so good. I love the Church, I love Christian leaders, and more importantly— God loves us. *"Dear God, you care about your people; please send us and renew Christian leaders to love your people and lead them into your Kingdom. Amen!"*

ACKNOWLEDGMENTS

Thanks to my wife who spent hours looking over my content, and was a great consultant for this book.

Thanks to all the pastors and Christian leaders who have influenced me greatly in ministry.

ABOUT THE AUTHOR

Brian's greatest joy in ministry is sharing the Gospel with others, seeing people's lives changed, and discipling others to pass on the faith. He received a Bachelor of Arts in Religious Studies with a minor in Communication from the University of Dubuque. He also attained a Master of Divinity from The University of Dubuque Theological Seminary. He has been the recipient of awards for preaching and church growth. Currently, he is the lead pastor of Well of Life, a church plant he and his family started in Hammond, Louisiana.

Brian can be contacted at:

P.O. Box 4014
Hammond LA, 70404
welloflifehammond@gmail.com
(985) 318-0687

www.ingramcontent.com/pod-product-compliance
Lightning Source LLC
Chambersburg PA
CBHW060752050426
42449CB00008B/1380